THE
ULTIMATE BOOK
OF SURVIVAL GEAR

THE ULTIMATE BOOK OF SURVIVAL GEAR

A BEGINNER'S GUIDE TO CHOOSING THE PRODUCTS THAT WILL KEEP YOU ALIVE

JAMES C. JONES

Skyhorse Publishing

Skyhorse Publishing books may be purchased in bulk at special discounts for sales promotion, corporate gifts, fund-raising, or educational purposes. Special editions can also be created to specifications. For details, contact the Special Sales Department, Skyhorse Publishing, 307 West 36th Street, 11th Floor, New York, NY 10018 or info@skyhorsepublishing.com.

Skyhorse® and Skyhorse Publishing® are registered trademarks of Skyhorse Publishing, Inc.®, a Delaware corporation.

Visit our website at www.skyhorsepublishing.com.

10 9 8 7 6 5 4 3 2 1

Library of Congress Cataloging-in-Publication Data is available on file.

Cover design by Mona Lin
Cover photo credit: James C. Jones

Print ISBN: 978-1-5107-5309-9
Ebook ISBN: 978-1-5107-6060-8

Printed in China

This book is dedicated to our ancestors, who were all survivalists and without whose survival instincts and perseverance we would not exist today, and to our descendants to whom we owe a determination to preserve life and freedom for the future.

Table of Contents

Introduction

In my previous books, *Advanced Survival, Total Survival,* and *150 Survival Secrets,* I focused on the psychological and skill-based aspects of survival and emergency preparedness. This volume is dedicated to the equipment and supplies needed to survive a wide range of emergency situations. Two of the most important principles of survival relate specifically to material equipment:

- **Have what you need:** This sounds simple, but it requires careful anticipation and awareness to have the right stuff where and when you need it. For example, having lots of food and firearms is not what you need when you have a house fire. You need good fire extinguishers! Having a full NBC suit and mask at home to protect against direct contact with a radioactive substance will not help in the more likely situation of you encountering smoke or biological hazards. It's not what you have, it's what you have with you that counts. Prioritizing and acquiring skills, supplies, and equipment based on your personal and realistic expectations—rather than popular media scenarios—is critical. The objective is to have safe air, effective defense, adequate shelter, clean water, sufficient food, required medical care, when and where you need it.
- **Use what you have:** The accumulation of stuff alone will not assure survival. You have to know how to use it and then use it effectively. You will also be faced with situations where you need to improvise and scavenge. Junk and scraps can be transformed into useful items. Nature provides food, shelter, fuel, and other necessities when we do not have other options. Survival training greatly increases your options and capabilities with and without stuff. In today's world we have

specially made products for every aspect of survival. This may make us complacent and dependent. A good exercise is to take every survival item you have and say "what if I had to do without this," then "what could I use in place of this." Know how to use it and know how to do without it, then you are a survivor!

The concept of survival gear as a category of equipment is fairly new. Prior to the late nineteenth century everything was "survival stuff" and a level of self-reliance and preparedness was the norm rather than the exception for most Americans. A knife, a gun, an axe, dried foods, stored water, and most of what we now consider "emergency preparedness" items were just normal supplies and tools. The evolution of grid-provided light, heat, water, food, protection, and emergency services, combined with the population shift to centralized urban and suburban residency, placed the majority of the population at risk and vulnerable to any large scale disaster or system failure. The "wonders" of technology and "big city life" were the dominant factors during the first half of the twenty-first century. The dawn of the nuclear age after World War II initiated the first interests in "survival" and having "survival gear." World War II also generated the development of survival training and survival equipment for downed pilots. The civilian was left with Civil Defense recommendations that only applied to surviving a nuclear holocaust and surplus military equipment and manuals such as *FM 21-76 Survival* that were of marginal utility for home emergency situations. Even "Be Prepared" Boy Scout manuals were more about camping than disaster preparedness.

The "survivalists" or "self-reliance practitioners" of the 1950s and 1960s, had to get by with military surplus, Boy Scout items, and a lot of homemade and improvised gear. It was not until the late 1970s that we began to see a few good civilian-related survival items on the market. The increasing frequency of natural and man-made disasters, terrorist acts, and potential system failures in the past few decades has generated a market for truly useful and high-quality survival items designed specifically for civilian use. As the narrow threat of nuclear war was replaced by a broad-range of potential emergencies and disasters, the variety and availability of equipment designed to save, preserve, and defend the lives of individuals and families through even the most challenging situations has grown into a major business market. Today's responsible citizen seeking to achieve a greater capacity to survive, escape, withstand, and recover has a wide range of products from which to choose.

In 2013, the American Housing Survey conducted by the US Census Bureau determined the level of emergency preparedness of American families. The results of such surveys can be considered "soft data," subject to how the respondents interpret the questions and their definitions of the wording. The survey indicated that fifty-four percent of Americans had at least twenty-four bottles of water for emergencies, whereas a bare minimum of five gallons per person is recommended. Eighty-two percent of respondents said that they had at least three days of food on hand for emergencies. In reality, most homes always have enough residual food, and leftovers for three days, but many emergencies require that at least a thirty day supply of non-perishable (canned, dried, dehydrated) foods be available. Fifty-one percent of those surveyed indicated that they had an emergency evacuation kit. How adequate these kits are or whether they had kits for every family member was not established. As the rate and severity of disasters has continued to escalate, we can hope that family preparedness levels improve.

Furthermore, existing equipment will need to be upgraded and updated to meet emerging challenges and hazards. In this book, I have provided options for those just starting their journey towards preparedness and those engaged in continuous improvement and advanced preparedness. This book explores each category of survival gear and emergency supplies with attention to their importance, functions, and options available. A variety of available products are illustrated with specifications, qualities, prices, and sources. Where possible, products of various price ranges and qualities are covered. While it is best to have only high-quality, high-end items in all these survival categories, everyone will have some budget limitations, so low-cost and surplus items are included wherever possible.

I have been collecting survival-related equipment for over fifty years and own multiple items for virtually every category, but it is not practical or affordable for me to include the latest and most expensive items in all categories. New products are coming onto the market even as I write this book and the reader is encouraged to consult websites, catalogues, and stores of the listed vendors (see appendix) to consider updated products. In Chapter 27, I bring these items together in a number of different configurations to meet different survival imperatives including short-term survival kits, evacuation packs, full survival or bugout bags, and home survival supplies.

While this book is dedicated to the material aspects of survival, emergency preparedness, and self-reliance, I must emphasize that knowledge, attitude, and the will to survive are more important than gear and supplies. In our materialist society we tend to believe that having "stuff" is the answer to all challenges, but you must have the right stuff in the right place at the right time and be willing and able to use it effectively to survive under high-hazard, high-stress conditions. The most important "survival stuff" is what's in your head.

About the Photographs in This Book

The majority of the photographs in this book are of my own survival gear. Having accumulated fifty years' worth of outdoor survival and emergency preparedness related equipment, it would be impractical and unaffordable to replace all of the older items with newer gear. No items were contributed by vendors or shown in exchange for material or financial contributions. Each photograph should be viewed with the following criteria in mind.

- All photographs are intended to illustrate a variety of examples and options within a category, but by no means do they include every variation.

- All photographs usually include a mixture of newer and older products. It was economically impractical to purchase the newest and most expensive items for each category.
- New survival and self-reliance products are being introduced every month, so newer versions of items shown may be available from vendors.
- All photographs do not necessary include every item described in the text.
- Some photographs include items that are no longer available, but provide examples of a type of item in that category.

Top row, left to right: World War II vintage field jacket, web-gear, and stainless steel canteen in insulated pouch with attached US Air Force survival knife; Rare US Army wool sleeping bag.

Middle row, left to right: US Army gasmask in bag, army blanket and army issue cooking mess pan, British Army ammo bag and surplus net-hammock.

Bottom row, left to right: US Army Military Police thirty-eight-caliber revolver, well-used army shovel, and an official Boy Scout knife.

Chapter 1
Early Survival Gear

Immediately after World War II, a large quantity of military surplus gear came onto the civilian market. Army Surplus Stores were a presence in virtually every community. Most of the military equipment used to fight in the Korean War during the 1950s was the same as that used by GIs in Europe during World War II in the 1930s and 1940s. However, the Korean War produced some improved winter gear.

In the early days of the decades-long Cold War between the United States and the Soviet Union, the only method of delivering nuclear bombs to Soviet targets was with bombers. It was assumed that any downed pilots would have to survive, escape, and evade in hostile territory, so the Air Force developed some high-quality survival kits and equipment. In addition to the excellent Air Force Survival Knife, they introduced the AR-7—a .22 long-rifle caliber, breakdown survival rifle with a floating stock. This weapon is currently sold by Henry Repeating Arms. The Air Force also issued the M6 folding Air Crew rifle that featured over-and-under twenty-two long-rifle caliber and .410 shotgun barrels. Unfortunately, the M6 was never offered to the civilian market. The most common survival-related surplus items available were packs, pup tents, jackets, canteens, mess-kits, knives, and web-gear. Weight was not a major factor in military specification, since they were designing items to be carried only by healthy young soldiers or transported in trucks.

The Vietnam War generated some equipment that was more adaptable to civilian, survival, and evacuation requirements. The Vietnam era ALICE (All-purpose, Lightweight, Individual, Carrying, Equipment) pack came in small, medium, and large sizes with padded straps, an aluminum frame, and multiple pockets. Surplus ALICE packs were the foundation for most early bugout bags. The bulky Army Shovel of the World War II era was replaced by the much lighter folding shovel in the 1970s.

Items designed for the backpacking, camping, and hunting markets also provided useable equipment for survival packs—at least until more suitable products became available. While the requirements for civilian survival and evacuation gear are significantly different than the requirements for recreational hiking and camping or for military operations, these were the primary sources for survival equipage until the introduction of purpose-built survival products for the civilian market in recent decades.

Chapter 2
Pocket and Belt Survival Gear

Always remember that it's not what you have, it's what you have with you that counts in a survival situation. You are most vulnerable when you are away from your home. You may be on the road or in town when a storm, civil disorder, terrorist attack, or other threat situation develops. You may find yourself in an active shooter location. You may be injured or the victim of a criminal assault. In most cases it is unlikely that you will have ready access to a complete survival kit or pack. In such emergencies you will have to depend on the items that you carry in your pockets, on your belt, or in your everyday emergency bag. The objective is to have the essential, short-term capacity to stay alive, escape the hazard, and signal for help in the first minutes of an emergency. Since most of the items you can easily carry with you are small and inexpensive, it is both practical and desirable to keep them in the pockets of every jacket and vest.

POCKET-SIZED RESPIRATORS

Fires, chemical spills, epidemics, bombing, earthquakes, and other disasters can strike without warning and create a toxic atmosphere. If you can't breathe or are breathing in toxic materials, your chances of survival decrease significantly. Carry an N95 fold-flat dust and mist respirator at all times. These can be purchased at any hardware store and provide protection against most biological agents, toxic particulates, and mists, as well as temporary protection from toxic chemicals. This respirator will not protect you from carbon monoxide or other toxic gases. However, a variety of man-made and natural disasters will produce smoke, soot, toxic dusts, and vapors, thus having respiratory protection in your pocket is a must.

If you are caught without your pocket-sized respirator, tying a bandana or clean cloth around your nose and mouth can block out some larger materials that you might breathe in otherwise.

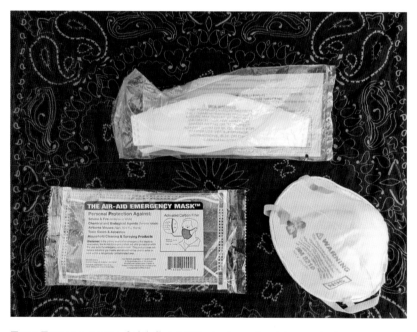

Top: Easy to carry, fold-flat N95 dust and mist respirator.
Bottom row, left to right: Air-Aid dust, mist, and chemical respirator, impregnated with activated charcoal to provide protection from hazardous chemicals; commonly available N95 dust and mist respirator available at hardware stores.
Background: A cloth bandana that can provide some protection from particulates.

Small Pocketknives

One useful survival mantra is "always carry a knife." Having a knife of any kind in your possession provides a tremendous advantage in any survival emergency. While you may want to have a small low-priced knife in every jacket to assure that you always have at least one knife, you should have a high-quality knife that you place in your personal carry items just like your wallet, keys, and cell phone.

Top row, left to right: Multi-bladed Swiss Army knife, small multi-tool.
Middle row, left to right: A rather large neck-knife in a pouch, modern Leatherman™ twenty-five function, the Leatherman™ Wave multi-tool. (Note that the Leatherman™ twenty-five function blade deploys without the need to open the pliers—the older Leatherman™ Wave multi-tool requires opening the pliers to access the blades and tools.)
Bottom row, left to right: Handy sized pocket knife, larger SOG folding knife with cord and seatbelt cutter.

You may be able to carry a large folding blade knife in casual clothing, but it is good to have a smaller pocket knife for dress up. Cargo pants usually have a pocket that fits a three-inch folding knife. Carrying a Swiss Army knife or multi-tool on your belt is the best option for casual dress. If you opt to carry a multi-tool, be sure to get one that has a knife blade that is accessible without you having to open the pliers. Don't skimp on expense for your primary carry knife, but also don't get fooled into paying too much just for a brand name. There are plenty of good quality knives available. Benchmade and Kershaw are high end choices, but Gerber, Ka-Bar, Smith and Wesson, Buck, Spyderco, and Victroninox offer good quality at a reasonable cost.

Some survivalists like to carry a "neck-knife" as a backup or out-of-sight knife. These are very small knives that hang on a cord or chain around the neck. They are generally available through knife-specialty outlets such as Blade Headquarters or Kershaw. While you cannot carry any kind of knife on an aircraft today, you can place them in your checked baggage to have at your destination.

FIRE STARTERS—MATCHES, LIGHTERS, AND STRIKERS

While the ability to start a fire is not critical in every survival situation, having a good lighter or a pack of matches can come in handy. Water-proof, windproof camp matches are better yet, or you can add a small magnesium fire striker to the items that you carry every day. The most economical strikers cost less than two dollars. Although strikers are reliable, they require some user skill and time, whereas matches and lighters provide a flame immediately.

MINIATURE LED FLASHLIGHT

While most folks carry a cellphone that provides some light, these can be lost or stolen. I recommend that you have a micro-flashlight on your key chain and another one in every coat pocket.

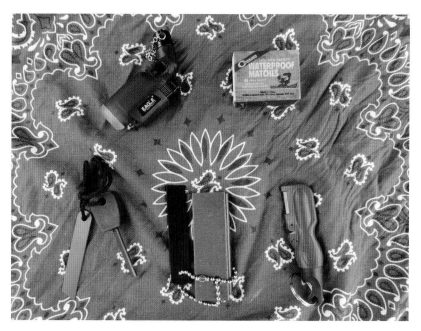

Pocket sized fire starters.
Top row, left to right: Torch-style cigarette lighter, windproof matches.
Bottom row: Three varieties of small magnesium spark striker devices.

A variety of available pocket and key chain flashlights.

Micro-flashlights come in a variety of sizes. I have at least a single-LED mini light in each jacket and four-LED lights in parkas and coats. Even the smallest LED light can give you a large advantage when the lights go out in the elevator or anywhere else, and for finding your way around or signaling for help.

WHISTLE

Disasters are noisy. There is crashing, banging, burning, screaming, and yelling. A piercing whistle has a much better chance of getting someone's attention than your voice. Whistles are cheap and small. There is no excuse for not having one in your pocket, on your keychain, or in your purse.

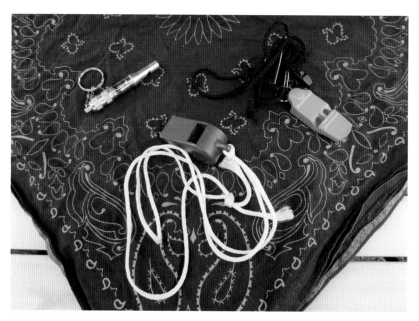

A few examples of small whistles to have with you.

Self-Defense Device — Firearm or Pepper Spray

Pepper spray devices are cheap and small enough for every key chain and pocket. Even if you legally carry a handgun on your person, it is essential to have options. Tasers require close contact, and are a bit larger than pepper spray, but if you have room in your pockets, that's an alternative. MACE is actually just another brand of pepper (OC) spray. Carrying pepper spray can allow you to feel safer as you travel or allow you to distract a threating person while you make your getaway in an emergency situation.

Responsibly handled handguns are my choice for the best personal defense device. While most states have some kind of open or concealed carry law, concealment is preferable in the case of being physically threatened by another person. Since the transgressor initiates violent acts, we can assume that he or she will look to attack those who are armed first before they can react. Let them be the surprised party, not you. The size of your carry gun depends on your ability to conceal it, but you certainly want to have a carry gun with stopping power and at least six shots. Full sized handguns are generally difficult to conceal and unnecessarily bulky for constant carrying. Remember: you're carrying the weapon to stop an attack or facilitate your escape, not to fight a war.

If you are going to carry a concealed firearm regularly, you will need a variety of carry devices and probably more than one weapon size. There are plenty of good inside-the-belt and outside-the-belt fast draw holsters that can secure your weapon out of sight under a loose T-shirt or jacket. There are also some great concealed-carry vests and jackets available. In warmer weather or casual situations in which a jacket is unnecessary, it is difficult to conceal a firearm in a belt holster of any kind. You probably need to consider owning an enclosed belt pouch or belted holster pouch. When asked what's in my personal belt pouch, I just say, "a wireless hand-held device." While pocket carry is not the best option, it sometimes is the only one. In such cases, a small six-shot, .380 caliber automatic padded

Top row, left to right: Fist enhancement device, heavy tactical pen, small electric stun-gun, pocket pepper spray.
Bottom row, left to right: .380 caliber, Ruger, auto-pistol: 9 millimeter Smith & Wesson Shield auto-pistol.

with a few bandanas for comfort—and to avoid the obvious handgun profile—is ideal. Although anything smaller than .380 caliber is of doubtful value in defensive action, they are far better than having nothing, therefore one of these is an option for when concealment is difficult.

First Aid Items

If you are dependent on medication of any kind, you should carry some with you at all times. You may be unable to get home or reach a pharmacy for a length of time during a major emergency. Heart medications, insulin, asthma medication, epinephrine for allergies, and daily medications must be easily at hand to ensure your continued safety.

While you can't conveniently carry a full first aid kit around with you, a few items will come in handy or even prove lifesaving in an emergency. If you are over fifty years old, then carrying a packet of aspirin at all times is important. Taking aspirin at the first sign of a heart attack can mean the difference between life and death. A few Band-Aids™ are handy for small cuts or repairs. A miniature bottle of alcohol-based hand sanitizer can clean wounds, prevent infections, and be used as fuel for a fire starter in an emergency. Depending on pocket space, you may want to carry a small tourniquet or hemostatic blood stopper gauze packet, but a bandana can be used almost as quickly.

BANDANAS

Bandanas were a must have in past centuries and should be carried by anyone seeking to be perpetually self-reliant today. Bandanas come in a variety of colors, are usually about twenty-two by twenty-two inches square, and cost less than three dollars each. They can easily be folded to fit inside any pocket. As I have mentioned throughout this chapter, bandanas have a wide range of useful purposes. A bandana can be quickly turned into an effective bandage, tourniquet, splint or sling, dust mask[1], head cover, short rope, carrying sack, flag to signal for help, and more. MacGyver could probably find another one hundred uses. Oh, and don't forget its use as a cleaning cloth and handkerchief. I recommend that you carry two, one red or yellow, and one dark or camouflage.

MEDICAL INFORMATION CARD

In an emergency, you may be seriously injured or incapacitated. In such cases, rescuers, medics, and others may need critical information

---

1 *Not nearly as good as the folding N95 mask for filtering out dust and small particles, but far better than nothing.*

about you in order to provide effective care and contact your family. You should always carry a bright orange or red card in an easy to find place on your person, such as in your wallet. This card should list your blood type; your emergency contact names and phone numbers; your doctor's name, hospital, and phone number; any medical conditions that you may have; any medications that you are using; and any medication to which you are allergic. Having this information immediately available for EMS personnel to access could save your life.

SPECIAL ITEMS AND SUBSTITUTIONS

There are dozens of pocket survival kits, cards, and gadgets on the market. Some combine whistles, flashlights, compasses, magnifiers, and other useful tools. Survival cards are generally flat, sharp pieces of stainless steel with various survival functions, such as cutting, open-

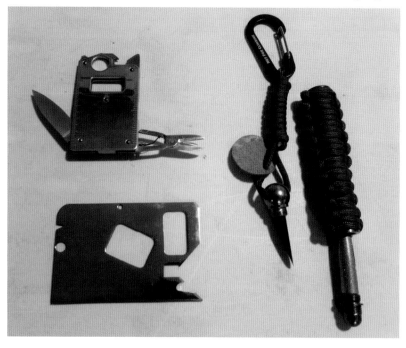

Left to right: Two versions of the wallet-sized survival card, "survival stick" key chain device.

ing, and signaling. These can be used to replace some, but not all of the items specified above or as backup pocket items. ReadyMan recently introduced a line of ultra-thin survival cards that are designed to be separated into various survival and escape devices. These fit easily into wallets and pockets.

Some folks think that having an app on a cellphone covers some of these needs and while that is okay for backup, technology can never be as reliable as actual tools and supplies. These technological devices and the aid that they are meant to bring to you are the most likely to fail just when you need them most. Real will always beat virtual.

Vests can be turned into self-contained survival kits. They have enough pocket space for a rain poncho, survival blanket, fire starters, and other survival essentials. Some vests are also designed to carry concealed firearms.

Chapter 3
Clothing and Footwear

What should the well-dressed survivor wear to a disaster? Of course, in most cases we won't know that we are headed toward a disaster, so we will probably find ourselves wearing clothing that is "appropriate" for our daily routine. That said, we can still select clothing that affords some advantages. Obviously, the more pockets the better. Cargo pants provide adequate room for the survival essentials enumerated in the previous chapter. You can wear a light-weight vest over a T-shirt in order to carry equipment and even conceal-carry weapons. Earth tones or neutral colored clothing are best in most cases, whereas camouflage patterned clothing now tends to attract attention in some urban environments.

Your everyday footwear may suddenly become survival footwear in an emergency. Avoid high heels, open-toed shoes, and sandals. If you can't avoid wearing these types of footwear, have a pair of full-foot covering shoes with you[2].

---

2   After the original World Trade Center bombing in 1993, the fire escape stairways were full of abandoned high heeled shoes. After that, most of the women in the buildings kept a pair of sneakers in their desk drawers. Quite a few also kept dust masks there as well. These precautions served them well on 9/11.

Always dress for what the weather could be, not just what it is outside at the moment. You may be surprised by a sudden temperature change or a rain storm. In a major emergency event, you may not be able to get home or into shelter for a while, so be prepared. A lot of outdoor clothing is made from cotton or cotton-blend material. Cotton is fairly durable, comfortable, and warm enough for mild to cool weather, but cotton loses most of its isolative value if it gets wet. Wool is heavier and can be hot and itchy in warm weather, but is a must for truly cold and wet conditions. Wool provides some insolation value even when it is wet. Winter socks, caps, and gloves should always be made of wool.

If you are engaged in outdoor activities, you can wear truly effective survival clothing, boots, hats, and carrying equipment. This is your disaster "turn-out" gear. This wardrobe can range from basic outdoor survival and camping cloths to military-like, combat gear. Durability and comfort are high priorities. Camouflage for the environment (urban or wilderness) and the season should also be considered. Most survival-oriented clothing includes plenty of pockets and attachment points for gear. Don't overlook the need for gloves and extra socks. I recommend keeping one complete set of survival clothing and boots with your bugout bag. You may not have time to find your clothing and get dressed in a severe emergency, so you can just grab your bag and clothes to dress properly later.

An essential rule of survival should always be "don't get wet." If you are in a survival situation, Murphy's Law will ensure that it rains or snows on you to add to your challenges. Getting soaked can lead to a variety of problems, including hypothermia. Once soaked, you can die of hypothermia even in mild temperatures. Wet clothing—particularly cotton—will drain your energy, just as if you were immersed in cold water. Additionally, survival items in your pockets and any survival gear you are wearing can become soaked and unusable. For these reasons, you should place a high priority on having effective and accessible rain gear. I recommend heavy-duty military rain ponchos for every survival kit and bugout bag. These should be kept on top of the pack for quick access. Cheap plastic ponchos are perfect for fitting in your pocket or purse. Rain suits are more comfortable than ponchos, but are not as versatile and offer no protection for your pack, weapon, or other gear. Ponchos can be worn over your pack and can also be rigged as shelters. Rain gear can also provide protection from chemical contaminants and radioactive fallout in the air when you combine it with respiratory and hand protection. Be sure to get a poncho long enough to hang well below your knees.

Top row, left to right: Russian-style heavy winter hat, Balaclava-helmet head cover and face mask, wool cap, warm weather "boone-cap."
Middle row, left to right: Wool mittens with glove fingers, leather combat gloves, work gloves for debris and glass.
Bottom row, left to right: White cotton socks, heavy wool socks, long winter socks. (Extra socks are a must in every kit and pack.)

Disposable Tyvek™ suits are available at most hardware stores and provide protection against chemical contamination, biological agent contamination, wind, rain and even radioactive fallout exposure when worn with an N95 dust and mist respirator. They are cheap and lightweight enough for any survival pack as a backup or replacement for your contaminated or wet clothing.

Gloves are often overlooked when individuals pack up their survival gear. A pair or two of latex medical gloves in your pockets can come in handy. Heavy-duty work gloves are a must for dealing with debris and rubble created by a disaster. Of course, warm winter gloves are also a must under cold conditions. Utility gloves are light or medium weight gloves that are designed for everyday hand protection. There are a wide variety of military surplus options, some of which can be supplemented with liners. Outdoor hunting gloves are also a good option, some of these include a trigger-finger opening. Tactical or combat gloves combine the flexibility of utility gloves with the toughness of work gloves. This is not surprising, considering these are the gloves designed for Military and SWAT teams. They are good for survival, but not for fine work such as making repairs, first aid, or tying cordage. You may want to consider wearing a heavy pair of gloves over a light pair to maintain protection through your various needs. Mittens are definitely an advantage for long-term exposure to extreme cold. They should be worn over light gloves and be kept on a string to prevent losing them. You should carry an extra pair of gloves under your shirt, in case the ones you are wearing become wet or lost. Another option is to have a pair of heavy wool socks under your shirt to replace wet socks or serve as emergency mittens. Your hands are your second most valuable survival tool, next to your brain, so you should select appropriate protection based on your anticipated hazards and task.

Regardless of what boots you select to keep with your survival gear, they should be comfortable and broken in. The last thing you need in an emergency is for your brand new boots to cause you pain and blisters when you need to keep moving to survive.

Those living in locations where winters can be severe must have clothing for a "worst case" winter survival situation. We normally live in heated homes, drive heated vehicles, and shop and work in heated environments. Thus, unless we are avid winter campers or hunters, our winter clothing and footwear is probably inadequate.

Left to right: Winter hunting boots, ideal for cold weather only; well-worn hiking shoes, good for general use, but are not water-proof; police boots, comfortable, durable, and ideal for urban and field movement.

Consider having to live in an unheated home wearing heavy sweaters and coats full-time. What if you have to evacuate during sub-zero, snow, cold rain, or even blizzard conditions? You will need layers of serious protection including insulated pants, snow suits, bala-clava face masks, and—most importantly—well-insulated boots and multiple pairs of winter socks. Fortunately, there are plenty of high-quality winter clothing options available at sporting goods stores and on the military surplus market. This is one area where you do not want to scrimp. Buy the best you can afford.

The old pioneer adage is that "if your feet are cold, put on your hat." A warm wool stocking cap should be included in every survival kit and pack. Even during mild weather such a cap can help con-serve your warmth on cool nights. Hooded garments are also helpful. For true winter conditions, hooded parkas or heavy winter caps with neck and ear-flaps are a must.

Top: Large pop-tent, too heavy for a survival pack, but could be carried in a vehicle.

Bottom, left to right: Tarp, can be easily carried and fashioned into various shelter configurations; smaller two-person tent, can be carried a short distance; cordage and fasteners, used with tarps; tarp.

Chapter 4
Shelters, Blankets, and Sleeping Bags

Securing shelter is often the first priority of survival. When we are forced to abandoned structural shelters or are caught outside during an emergency, we must depend on portable and efficient shelter equipment.

TENTS

In some cases shelters may be sufficient tents, while in other cases we may have to use tarps and plastic sheeting to improvise a sturdy shelter. You should include a lightweight tent with rain-flies in a full-sized survival backpack, but you may be limited to tarp-like shelters or compact survival tents with a smaller survival kit. There are very compact, pocket-sized, two person, Mylar survival tents such as the Trail Blazer™ that sell for as little as seven dollars. Such small tents are sold by survival supplies outlets, but you may find them at camping stores as well. They are perfect for survival kits and evacuation packs, but are only durable enough to last a few days.

The primary function of a shelter is to keep wind, rain, and snow out, while keeping heat in. One often overlooked application of a tent is for in-home use in the event of a long-term, cold weather grid failure. While it might be impossible and hazardous to heat the entire house, setting up a tent inside of the home and just heating that with small tent-heaters is much more practical. For survival purposes, a shelter should be big enough for comfort, but not so big that you cannot conserve body heat. In general, the tent should be one person size larger than the number of occupants that will occupy it. (Use a "three person" tent for two occupants.) Any evacuation pack or bugout bag must include some form of shelter to effectively ensure your survival.

BLANKETS AND SLEEPING BAGS

Even in the mildest weather, it is essential to have some form of protection and heat conservation while sleeping. Fortunately, there are a wide range of blankets and sleeping bags available to meet every need. An emergency may either involve sheltering in place without adequate heat (electric or gas) or evacuating into the elements with just what you can carry. If you are sheltering at home, weight and bulk are not an issue, but since we are accustomed to heated homes, we may not have adequate blankets or sleeping bags for prolonged, winter survival. If you are an active backpacker, you can certainly carry a high-quality sleeping bag in or on your bugout bag. However, if your carrying capacity is limited to a smaller survival pack or evacuation bag you may need to settle for a lighter bag or blanket.

Very lightweight, Mylar™ blankets and bags can easily fit into packs or even pockets. These offer decent heat conservation and rain protection, but are rather fragile and last only a day or two. There is a full range of blanket and bag options in a wide range of weights and prices available for sale. I recommend weatherproof sleeping bag covers. You can also opt for a "sleep system" that includes a sleeping bag, liner, and outer "bivy shelter" that replaces the need for a tent. It

Left to right: Army surplus wool sleeping bag; Army surplus goose feather, medium, cold weather sleeping bag; (on top of center bag) Stealth Angle light-weight, compacted sleeping bag, good for cool weather only; very small, three ounce Mylar™ emergency sleeping bag; more durable Titan Survival Emergency sleeping bag; (right) commercial cold weather sleeping bag inside of a camouflage, Gore-Tex™, bivy-sack can be used without a tent if necessary.

Top row, left to right: Three versions of aluminized Mylar™ survival blankets, intended for short-term (one to three days) emergency use; much more durable Space Blanket™, an absolute essential in every survival pack.
Bottom row, left to right: The classic, wool Army blanket, cheap, durable, and warm; tough, waterproof, heavy "tactical blanket."

is critical to select the combination of shelter, bag, and blanket that's right for you, your climate, and your anticipated situation. If you anticipate being outside during a Northern winter, do not scrimp on what you spend on a sleeping bag. Check the rating and err on the side of caution. If you anticipate that the coldest nights you will encounter will be ten degrees above zero, get a bag rated at least ten degrees colder.

Cheaper bags with synthetic insulation are fine for home or vehicular evacuation, but are usually heavier and bulkier than down-filled bags rated for the same temperatures. Truly warm, light, and compressible bags are more expensive, but are a must if you anticipate evacuation and carrying your bag and survival gear under winter conditions. Good surplus bags are available for fifty to one hundred dollars. Commercial bags and sleep systems can cost from as little as eighty to as much as $500. The best guidelines are to purchase the best sleeping bag you can afford and the most heavy-duty bag that you can carry.

Chapter 5
Knives, Axes, Shovels, and Saws

KNIVES

Today, virtually everyone uses some kind of knife at least a few times each day, whether for eating, in a work setting, or for a recreational hobby. If you possess a knife, you instantly have a huge survival and self-defense advantage. Even if you have nothing else with you, a knife still gives you a chance to survive. Not carrying a knife of some kind is surrendering your survival potential to luck and the whims of nature and other people. The prepared person will carry a pocketknife or a pouch knife throughout the day. He or she may also keep a larger "survival knife" or "hunting knife" in their vehicle or other accessible location.

Of course, there will be well-selected small and large blades for outdoor activities that you can keep stashed in the survival or evacuation pack. You may carry a heavy-bladed six- to eight-inch blade-length belt knife for heavy work. A small thin-bladed pocketknife for fine work and maybe a Swiss Army™ type knife or multi-tool with a variety of blades and gadgets may prove useful to you as well. Some multi-tools even have an LED flashlight included. Some "survival knives" come with a match compartment in the handle and a compass in the butt. These are good for backup caches or extra knives, but most of these types of knives are weakened by the hollow handle and may break during heavy use.

You may want to consider one of the military bayonet knives that work with their sheath in order to cut wire. Traveling cross-country in most areas will mean you might be crossing a lot of wire. The M9 and M10 and the AK47 bayonets have wire cutters. Small sharpening stones are often included in a pouch right on the sheath, which I highly recommend. The knife is *not* the item on which to spend cheaply! A blade that goes dull or breaks when you need it the most is no bargain, but there are over-priced knives for which you are paying for a specific style or name. I am not talking about knife collecting or knife show knives in which your personal preferences can take precedent over functionality. For survival purposes, you need a reliable use and abuse blade. Ultimately, you have to select your knife set based on as much quality as you can afford. Survival and self-reliance knives can be classified as pocketknives, pouch knives, sheath knives, and combat knives. The following are some recommended selections from several knife experts.

Pocketknives are single or multi-bladed knives that fit into your pocket comfortably and unobtrusively, hence the name. In the past, almost everyone carried a pocketknife or "pen knife" to sharpen quill pens, clean pipes, and perform other daily tasks. For our purposes a pocketknife is a single or double-bladed knife of no more than three-inch blade length. You want this knife to be thin and light so you can carry it comfortably at all times, but you also want it to be strong and sharp. Some good choices are the Spyderco Native™ folder at about seventy-eight dollars, the Kershaw Combo Edge™ folder at about twenty-five dollars, and the Gerber Mini Covert™ folder at thirty-six dollars. The Smith and Wesson S.W.A.T™ frame lock folder and Black Ops™ folder priced in the twenty-five to thirty-five dollar range are good values as well. If you want more than one blade, the Swiss

Top row, left to right: Cheap, but useful, multi-bladed pocket knife; Swiss Army knife.
Middle row, left to right: Small single blade pocket knife; large single blade pocket knife.
Bottom row: Two larger, heavy-duty pocket knives, both with seat belt cutters and belt clips. The left knife also has a built-in solar-charged single LED flashlight.

Army™ Soldier knife (the original Swiss Army knife) with a blade, can opener, bottle opener, two screwdrivers, and an awl point fits in the pocket and costs about twenty-five dollars.

Pouch knives are those that are carried in a pouch or may be kept in other places, but are too large for comfortable pocket carrying. This includes large folders, Swiss Army knives, and multi-tools. If your normal apparel is work clothes or blue jeans you may be able to wear a belt pouch without attracting any negative attention. This provides the opportunity to carry larger and more versatile knives. However, things get more complicated here because you have to choose between one big, strong blade with limited uses or several smaller blades and tools with multi-use capabilities. In the multi-tool category there is the Leatherman New Wave™ tool with over a dozen functions at seventy-five dollars, the Gerber™ Diesel multi-tool at fifty-three dollars, and scores of other models to meet your requirements. Some even include LED flashlights, fire starters, whistles, and magnifying glasses. The drawback to the multi-tool concept is that the primary tool is usually a pliers rather than a knife blade, and getting to the knife blade is a bit slow and troublesome. Once deployed, the knife blade of a multi-tool is rather clumsy to use compared to a folder knife. You may still want or need to carry a pocketknife along with the multi-tool. The Swiss Army knife is a knife first and a tool second— the traditional Swiss Army™ knife also offers a great variety of choices. The ones with six to eight blades and devices are more compact and easier to use than the puzzle-like multi-tools. The Swiss Army™ Ranger with its twenty tools is a good choice for about forty dollars or you can go all out for the huge (and clumsy) Champ™ selling for close to eighty dollars. Some have twenty to thirty tools, but are bulky and awkward. Avoid cheap imitations. Stick with brand names and be sure of a good strong pouch that will not tear or come off your belt. Large folders with blades of about four inches offer the blade of a sheath knife in a more compact form, but they cannot be as strong for some applications. Consider the KA-BAR Mule™ folder at about forty-eight dollars or one of the popular Buck brand large folding knives.

Sheath knives are larger sheath carried blades ranging from the five inch blade US Airforce Survival Knife and the six inch blade US Marine Ka-Bar (also known as the Mark 1 utility knife) to machete lengths of twelve inches and more. The actual military surplus US Airforce Survival Knife and US Marine Ka-Bar are good values at about forty dollars, but KA-BAR brand makes an assortment of Ka-Bar variations selling in the fifty to sixty dollar range. Smith & Wesson offers the Ka-Bar-like Search and Rescue™ sheath knife with an excellent sheath and sharpening stone for under thirty dollars. Many people identify with the Rambo-style, hollow handled survival knife that contains various survival items within the handle, but most of

Left photo, Top: Classic Marine, Ka-Bar knife.
Middle: Commercial survival knife.
Bottom: US Airforce survival knife. Many knives come with a sharpening stone in the sheath.

Right photo: There are many versions of the hollow handled survival knife on the market, but this one seems to be the most complete and versatile. The solid six inch, stainless steel blade is hardened to Rockwell c 55/58 to take and hold sharpness and has a sawblade back. The solid, carbon-fiber sheath is wrapped in a significant amount of cordage and has a fold-out slingshot. The inner compartment of the sheath contains the slingshot bands, a small signal mirror, and a little skinning knife. Unscrewing the end of the sheath provides access to a compass and a cup that holds matches, slingshot ammunition, Band-Aids™, a scalpel blade, tweezers, a sewing and suture kit, and a fishing kit.

these knives are weaker, because the blade is secured to the handle by a pin rather than extending the full length of the handle. While I would not recommend these as primary survival knives, some are fairly durable in general. Chris Reeves make a hollow handled survival knife with a fully integral blade and handle, but it costs several hundred dollars. For value and quality there are several good options among military bayonets. The M-9 and M-10 are good choices.

Knives of over fourteen inches in overall length become impractical for most folks to carry on a belt sheath. If you anticipate some serious chopping and hacking you may want to consider carrying a heavy bladed knife in or across the back of your pack. Consider the Ontario RTAK-II™ bush knife with its ten inch blade and seventeen inch overall length for about ninety dollars or even a military surplus Machete on the market for as little as twenty dollars.

Combat knives are those specially designed for fighting. They are not usually ideal for other survival uses. These range from small concealable three inch blades and throwing knives to boot knives and commando knives. While knife fights are possible, they are not probable, so put survival knives ahead of combat knives in your purchasing and packing decisions. In certain situations and urban environments, a well-hidden combat knife could be just what you need. You may want to add something like the OSS Spike dagger that is carried on the wrist or the Special Ops™ five inch blade boot knife selling for about twenty-four dollars. There are variations of the famous Applegate-Fairbairn™ World War II style combat knives selling for from fifty to one hundred dollars. There are also small neck knives that hang around the neck in a sheath. They are inconspicuous and a handy, last-resort, backup blade.

Top row, left to right: Combat knife, designed for slashing; Karambit combat knife, designed for slashing (larger versions of the Karambit knife are sharp on both sides and practically impossible to defend against).
Bottom: Applegate-Fairbairn commando knife, designed for stabbing, but poorly suited for general survival use.

Neck Knives

"Always carry a knife" is a survivalist mantra. If you have nothing else, any kind of blade can still provide a big advantage in many survival situations. Large sheath knives are great for outdoor activities and survival gear that you would wear during evacuations or disaster situations. Good pocket knives are a must for everyday casual wear and travel. The Swiss Army™ knife or various versions of the Leatherman™ multi-tool can usually be worn on small belt pouches or pockets without attracting too much attention. However, dress up occasions can prove a challenge for carrying a knife. Dress pants and suit jackets offer limited pocket space and even a small knife may imprint visibly through thin material. A neck knife can be worn unobtrusively under a dress shirt and even better hidden under a shirt and tie. While the small one or two inch blade has limitations,

Neck knives come in a variety of sizes, from the two inch blade on the left to the three inch blade on the right.

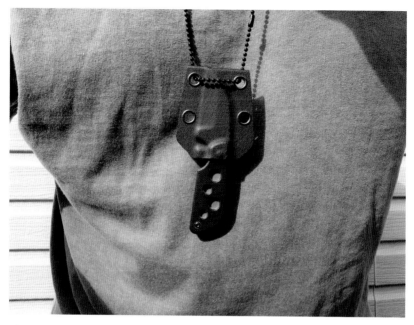

The neck knife is normally worn under a T-shirt and dress shirt together, not outside as shown here. It will be too noticeable if you wear it beneath a T-shirt alone.

it is far better than having no blade at all. Neck knives can be found online and at gun and knife shows for from ten to thirty dollars.

Even if you are able to carry a larger knife, the neck knife can serve as a backup blade in case your primary knife is lost or confiscated.

Knife Care and Safety

Leaving knives out is an invitation for trouble. They can be lost, stolen, damaged, picked up by children, or even used against you. Keep them in their sheath or pouch and in a safe location when not in use. Clean and lightly oil multi-blade knives so that they open freely when you need them. Knives are not intended for prying or hammering. Keep your knives sharp and clean. There is a wide variety of sharpening stones and sharpening devices available. Some knives come with a small sharpening stone in the sheath. Cabela's offers a wide variety of electric and hand-held sharpeners ranging in price from twenty to $400. You can get a good diamond stone for thirty to sixty dollars from Best Sharpening Stone, and these come with instructions. The Edgemaker™ sharpening system devices range from ten to thirty dollars and are handy for fast restoration of a blade.

Your choice of a knife system will depend on your anticipated everyday uses and your worst-case emergency needs. No one knife will be the best for every situation. You should have at least one high-quality pocketknife, multi-bladed pouch knife, and sheath knife, and carry all three if possible when in a potential survival threat situation. Cheaper backup knives stashed in various locations (e.g. vehicle, office, pack, etc.) will be far better than nothing if you are unable to access your primary blade. In some cases, what you want and what you can legally and practically carry will be a compromise, but I recommend to always carry a knife.

AXES, MACHETES, AND HATCHETS

Survival axes are not an "everyday carry" item, but can be a useful addition to survival gear and packs, depending on the anticipated survival challenges. Urban survival and escape situation may require breaking into buildings, chopping through walls or fences, and removing obstructions. Rural and wilderness survival can necessitate shelter building, wood cutting, and other tasks beyond the capability of knives or machetes. The leverage and power of hatchets that are specifically designed for survival and rescue can be what you need. There is a wide variety of axes, machetes, and hatchets available from several sources, ranging from full-length axes to short hatchets. There are dozens of quality manufacturers of axes, including Gerber, Columbia River, and Special Ops Gear (SOG), which tend to be more combat and survival-oriented in their designs with a "survival hatchet" that includes a magnesium fire starter at around forty dollars and Voodoo Hawk Mini™ at just thirty-four dollars. These devices are thin-bladed and lighter than traditional camp axes,

Top to bottom: SOG Voodoo Hawk™ survival hatchet; Combination hatchet, bush-hook, and shovel; Gerber, ten inch machete with saw blade back.

but are fully capable survival and rescue tools. Heavy-bladed, short machetes can be used for light chopping and sawing as well.

SHOVELS

A shovel is one of the items that is often left out of the bugout bag, but should be included if at all possible. Shovels have somewhat limited use in urban areas where an axe or pry bar may be more helpful, but they are incredibly useful once you leave the brick and concrete of the cities behind. Uses include digging shelters, digging fire pits, burying waste, drainage trenching, building defensive positions, and making animal traps. You may need to clear ground and shovel snow for cold weather camps as well.

There are a variety of small "camp shovels" on the market. Your choice depends on how much weight you can add to your survival pack. The two main designs are a miniaturized version of the old M-1951 Army Shovel or the current tri-fold designs. If you are really pressed for space and weight, a good quality garden trowel gives you at least some digging capacity. Some designs include a pick or saw blade. Of course you may want a bigger shovel in your vehicle or survival cache.

Top to bottom: Basic army shovel, good, but too heavy for survival packs; military folded shovel, very compact for campers; folding shovel; combination shovel and hatchet.

SAWS

While it may be impractical to carry a single-purpose sawblade, including a saw blade as part of a machete, knife, or shovel can be helpful in many survival and rescue tasks including shelter building and trap making. You may also want to consider the very compact stainless steel, survival wire saws such as the Survival Ring Saw at just under ten dollars or the UST Wire Saw at less than four dollars. These are small enough to fit into any survival kit or pack.

A typical wire saw costs less than five dollars and fits into any survival kit. They are available online or at most sporting goods and survival supply outlets.

Chapter 6
Stoves and Cooking Gear

The image of a survivor cooking over an open fire is iconic. Depending on your capacity to gather suitable fuel and start a fire under survival conditions, this idea can be problematic at best. Heavy rain, snow, and high winds can drown a fire even if you get one started. Spending time in the cold rain and wind gathering fuel can suck more energy out of you than you can gain by being warmed by and cooking over a fire. Fires are smoky and attract unwanted attention and can also cover your cooking gear with soot.

STOVES

A campfire may be practical under some conditions, but a stove gives you the capacity to quickly heat food and melt snow without exposing yourself to the elements. Consuming heated food and beverages is a much more efficient method of heating the body's core than sitting next to an open fire. There is a large variety of compact and efficient field stoves ranging from the ubiquitous German army, Esbit™ stove that burns cheap fuel tablets and costs under ten dollars, to a more costly mountaineering stove that burns Butane and costs between twenty to fifty dollars. The propane burning "pocket stoves" are certainly lighter, more compact, and efficient than liquid fuel burners, but it may be difficult for you to find additional fuel cartridges after a long-term emergency, while gasoline and kerosene may still be available. Another option is alcohol burning or Sterno™ stoves. They are cheap, clean burning, and their fuel is likely to be more available. Many of these stoves come as part of a cooking kit that includes a pot and a cup. I have found that it is more efficient to have a pocket stove and extra fuel in my bugout bag than self-heating MRE's.

It is certainly practical to carry some form of mini-stove and fuel for survival situations that will last a week or longer, but if your situation outlasts your stove's fuel supply, you may be left with a camp fire as your only option. One alternative to this is to have a rocket stove. Rocket stoves burn twigs and small branches more efficiently than an open fire. While you still have to find fuel, a few handfuls of twigs is easier to gather than branches and logs. A good rocket stove will fry an egg or boil a small pot of soup with just a few handfuls of twigs. While they are smokier and less convenient than tablet, propane, and liquid burning stoves, fuel is virtually unlimited and easy to find and keep dry. Rocket stoves are bulkier and not practical for a first choice unless you anticipate an extended or indefinite survival situation in the outdoors.

Larger one or two burner stoves such as those sold by Colman are great for home preparedness. These stoves cost between fifty and eighty dollars and should be kept with a stock of eight to twelve propane cylinders for emergency use.

Cooking Gear

When we think about survival, we seldom consider pots and pans. Your capacity to prepare hot food is an important element to your survival. While cold rations and energy bars are adequate for short term evacuation and survival situations, preparedness for anything over two or three days should include basic cooking equipment.

Top row, left to right: Primus gasoline stove; Dietz, Warm-it-Up™ combination lantern and stove; collapsible Sterno™ stove; High-tech, twig-burning, BioLite™ rocket stove; Colman LP gas stove.
Bottom row, left to right: Vintage kerosene expedition stove; basic World War Two Esbit™ stove; more advanced Esbit™ stove with integral cooking pot; surplus Swiss Army rocket stove; mini MRS LP-gas stove.

Typical, two burner LP gas camp stove, a must for home survival preparedness.

Since you are going to have to carry your kitchen, consider the weight and size of your gear as you make your selections. Your household utensils are not an option. Fortunately, there is a plethora of good choices from military surplus, Boy Scout, and backpacking suppliers. There are several "cooking systems" that include a mini-stove and nested pots and cups that take up little room. Some military pans are designed for a field kitchen or for cooking over an open fire and thus are not practical for survival situations. Your equipment should be usable over a small fire, but a mini-stove and extra fuel or a twig-burning rocket stove is the best option for the bugout bag. Don't forget your eating utensils! An Army surplus nested utensil set, Swiss Army-like spoon and fork, or even the often-maligned Spork will beat eating with your hands.

A variety of cooking kits and utensils. Note the German Army cooking kit is in the upper right hand corner, the US Army canteen cup in the middle, the popular Sierra™ cup in the lower left corner, and the Spork™ in the middle of the front row.

Chapter 7
Food for Kits and Homes

While it is generally accepted that a person can survive for several weeks without food, the effects of malnutrition and hunger start to degrade an individual's survival capacity within a few days. Progressive weakness, poor decision making, and lowered immunity are common effects of hunger. High stress situations and exposure to cold weather can exacerbate and accelerate the effects of malnutrition.

KITS AND PACKS

Short-term evacuation packs and survival kits should include high-energy, easy to use foods such as energy bars, nuts, candy, and granola. Full bugout or survival packs should include more substantial meals designed for campers and the military that can be eaten as-is or heated over a fire or camp stove. Self-heating meals and self-heating MREs (meals ready to eat) are designed for the military and backpacking, but are not ideal for survival packs. One or two MREs may be included to eat as a fast meal when cooking is impractical, but most evacuation and survival pack foods should be freeze-dried, dehydrated meals that can be reconstituted with hot water from a campfire or mini-stove. These provide more nutrition per pound and per cubic inch in your pack. A short-term evacuation pack should have only cold-edible, energy food, while a full bugout bag should contained a few days' worth of such foods and another four-to-six days' worth of full, dehydrated meals and a stove, fuel, and utensils to prepare them.

With the exception of the lifeboat rations at the top right, all of these foods are available at most grocery and convenience stores. They are high protein, high energy, and long shelf-life rations. These items are ideal for inclusion in Get Home Packs, Outdoor Survival Kits, and Three Day Evacuation Packs. They can supplement more substantial meals in a true Survival or Bugout Pack. The energy drinks in the middle of the top row would be essential if you need to stay awake and alert through an emergency. The Tootsie Rolls are an example of hard-candy, pocket food. They don't spoil or freeze and were the only food the Marines had to survive on when surrounded at the Choshin Reservoir in Korea between November 26 and December 11, 1950.

The general rule for food supplies per person is: three days for escape, six to eight days for a full bugout, and at least fifteen to thirty days for sheltering-in-place. Of course, the longer you can survive without outside sources of food and water the better. Vendors like Nitro-Pak offer a complete line of home-emergency food packages ranging from four to five days for about $700, to a full years' food supply for $3,500. Montana House brand is the most well-established source for freeze-dried survival foods. Their products are available at most camping and survival supply outlets. You can purchase Montana House meals individually or in pre-packaged multi-day kits. A three day package costs sixty-nine dollars and a five day package runs $115. Freeze-dried meals are expensive, but are very lightweight, take up little room, and have an extremely long shelf-life. If you can't afford to invest in several months' worth of food all at once, you can just set a goal to add a week's worth of storable food each month, every month until you reach your goal.

Food for Home and Retreats

Every home should have sufficient food to last from several weeks up to at least a month without access to grocery stores. Rotating canned goods and stocking up on non-perishable staples such as pasta, beans, and nuts is the most practical solution if you have room. There are plenty of long-lasting, freeze-dried meals specifically designed for emergency uses that take up little room, but will require you to store more water to reconstitute them. I recommend a combination of short-term energy food, freeze dried, portable meals, and home-stored canned goods and non-perishables for a balanced program. Home-stored survival foods should be kept in high-quality tote bins in a dry, safe location. Each tote bin should be light enough to carry. In an emergency, you may need to remove these from your home or place them in your vehicle quickly. You should list and inspect the contents of each tote quarterly. Canned goods should be rotated every few years. Building up a six month or one year's

Food storage choices depend on your budget and available storage space.

Left to right: A tote bin full of MREs, a selection of freeze-dried meals; pre-packaged thirty day food buckets from the NRA Store and Cabela's; vacuum-packed cans of emergency food from Emergency Essentials™.

If you need to upgrade your food supplies in a hurry, purchasing a prepackaged food bucket like this is an option. They are available from most survival supply vendors including Cabela's, the NRA Store, and ReadyWise™ (pictured) which cost $279, and provide 124 meals.

supply can be expensive, but budgeting to add a week's supply every month is practical and affordable for most families. Wise Company sells packages of freeze-dried survival meals with a twenty-five-year shelf life, as do Nature Essentials and Mountain House. MREs are complete meals that include coffee, entrees, drink mixes, and snacks. They are bulkier than other freeze-dried meals, but more compact and convenient than canned goods. A case of MRE Star™ MREs with twelve meals sells for eighty-five dollars.

Back row, left to right: Battery powered lantern, charged by a crank handle; battery powered lantern; classic Aladdin oil lamp, perfect for long-term home lighting; high-tech lamp that uses heat from a tea-candle to generate electricity for multiple LED bulbs; Colman LP gas lantern; classic kerosene lantern; selection of camping candles and tea-candles, reliable and cheap light sources.

Front row: Two versions of small, solar-powered lanterns.

Chapter 8
Lights, Batteries, and Chargers

FLASHLIGHTS AND LANTERNS

The technology for providing light has greatly improved since the early days of emergency preparedness. Back in the sixties, we still had bulky, D-cell flashlights with a single bulb, and oil or white gas lanterns. I still have my first single LED flashlight that cost twenty-seven dollars. Today, we have a wide variety of multi LED flashlights and lanterns, many of which are rechargeable from solar cells or crank generators. Whereas my old flashlight was good for a few hours of light on the batteries, modern LED flashlights and lanterns can go for several days without recharging. While cellphone screens and flashlights are useful for short-term situations, they are only good so long as the phone battery is charged.

Newer lighting devices are also not as heavy or large as old devices for comparable light output. Keychain lights are the size of a coin and as bright as my old flashlight. Other flashlights range from pen-sized to the size of a lipstick. Low cost, highly efficient lighting devices are available for every kind of camping and emergency use. Additionally, there are luminescent items that recharge when exposed to light and

Left to right: Mini LED flashlight; high-powered, tactical flash-light; small, solar-charge flashlight; high-tech, emergency responder flashlight with multi-colored lights; multiple power levels, mini-Maglite™; full sized Maglite™.
Back: UV Paqlite™ glow sheet, recharges from sunlight and provides useful illumination all night.

chemical light—Light Sticks™ for short term emergency light. A mini-light should be an everyday carry item. High powered, tactical flashlights with multi-level illumination settings are a must for evacuation and bug-out bags. Larger flashlights and rechargeable lanterns should be kept in every home and vehicle. Check these lights monthly and recharge them as needed. There is no excuse for being in the dark in any situation.

BATTERIES AND CHARGERS

While many devices self-recharge on attached solar cells, I advise having extra rechargeable batteries and a separate charging device.

You may need to leave the light on for an extended period of time or weather conditions may preclude recharging. Recharging one set of batteries while another is in use has many advantages. Charging devices can also be used to power cellphones, radios, and other essential communication equipment. There are many solar-powered battery chargers on the market that are small enough for the bugout bag and home use. Larger fold-out solar power devices can be used at home for auxiliary power and recharging.

Top row: Large solar panel, ideal for recharging many devices and comes with a variety of connections. **Bottom row, left to right:** Small solar charger, can be used to recharge cellphones and other small devices; portable solar battery charger, can charge rechargeable batteries.

Twenty-five pound CamelBak™ survival pack.

Chapter 9
Packs

The pack you select can greatly impact how much you can comfortably carry and how far you can carry it. Early survival packs were very basic World War II, GI, or Boy Scout style rucksacks. This was a simple, square canvas bag with a flap and shoulder straps—there was no padding, no external ties, and no compartments. You had to organize your equipment well in order to have what you needed on top.

Serious backpacking packs consist of a tall aluminum frame and bag that have plenty of places to secure sleeping bags and tents. They have wide, padded shoulder straps and a padded waist belt. These bags are great for backpacking, but not ideal for survival situations. The Vietnam-era medium ALICE pack with its light aluminum frame, padded straps, and low-profile was the best available pack for survival and evacuation in the 1970s and still is a good choice. There are also small ALICE packs and large ALICE packs available on the surplus market. Prices range from fifty dollars to $125. There is a wide selection of packs on the market today that can meet the needs of emergency evacuation or full bugout and survival situations.

Left photo: My current pack has well-padded shoulder straps, waist belt, and back. Your comfort should be a major consideration when you are selecting a pack.

Right photo: Two similar, military-style packs. These packs have plenty of compartments and well-padded straps, and cost about sixty dollars each.

Survival bags intended to get you through one or two days of basic needs (water, shelter, food, and rescue) can be simple daypacks or even heavy-duty fanny packs. Evacuation bags can be small backpacks with just shoulder straps, but true bugout and survival packs need to be large, with wide, well-padded shoulder straps and kidney (belt) straps to ensure comfort for long-distance carrying. This pack should have plenty of large outer compartments and tie-down straps for extra gear. I recommend a long "tear drop" shaped bag that conforms to the profile of your body. This shape will not interfere with your movement through tight areas in an urban or wilderness environment. A pack that rides high and hangs low from the back will pull on your shoulders and put you off balance. The definition of "camouflage" is that which is not noticed. In an urban environment a black, gray, or tan bag—like many students carry—would attract less attention than a military camouflage pack. Even good-quality, wheeled luggage with carry straps might work in urban environment. Just as long as it does

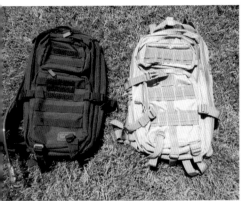 

Left photo: These military-style "assault packs" are strong and compact, ideal for evacuation packs and get-home bags, but too small for long-term survival. The one on the left has an internal water bladder and drinking tube.

Right photo: Small fanny packs like these are good for field survival kits where only short-term survival, escape, and rescue are the priorities.

not scream "survival pack!" In the far suburban and rural areas, a true camouflage pattern may be common and work best for your needs.

Fortunately, there is a virtually unlimited selection of packs available for sale that feature expandable compartments, tie-downs, nets, and partitions. Someone carrying a backpack or even a camouflaged backpack does not attract much attention in today's society. Select your pack based on what you absolutely must carry and what you actually are capable of carrying for a distance. Too large a bag will tend to encourage overloading, while too small a bag will force you to leave out items that you may need. Ultimately all your other gear depends on being carried and protected by the pack, so select yours with care and go for quality over economy.

Typical small concealed-carry handguns in .380 caliber and 9mm.

Chapter 10
Defense Weapons

Constant vigilance and tactical thinking can avoid most, but not all, confrontations with violent persons. Obviously, you should avoid combat and physical struggle with one or more assailants when possible, but when faced with someone who is determined to do you harm, you must have every possible advantage.

Urban Defense Weapons

Urban weapons can be divided into two categories: close-contact weapons that are used in physical contact with the assailant, and stand-off weapons that are effective at some distance from the assailant. Close-contact weapons include fist-enhancement devices, tactical pens, batons, knives, and Tasers. These devices are last-resort options because they involve struggling with a probably stronger person who may be able to deflect or even ignore the device. You are almost certain to sustain some injury in such a confrontation. Knives are seldom a good option for defense. You might not have access to your knife or have the time to open it while defending yourself in close quarters. A struggle with a knife usually results in injury to both parties. If displayed early, they may deter an attack, but they may also result in the assailant deploying their own knife or gun.

Stand-off weapons include pepper spray—an Oleoresin Capsicum (OC) device—and handguns. While both tools can be used while in direct contact with an aggressor, their main advantage is that they can deter or disable the assailant before contact. Handguns trump all other urban defense options since in your worst case scenario your opponent has a firearm and you are equal, while against all other weapons and even multiple assailants you have the advantage.

While open carry is legal in many states, it is not advisable. How large of a handgun you can comfortably conceal depends on your body size and clothing. I don't advise carrying a gun in your pocket or under your belt. A gun in the pocket will cause a visible imprint or cause the garment to sag on that side. Holsters specifically designed for belts and pockets can help you to avoid some of these draw-backs. There is a wide range of concealed-carry jackets, vests, purses, and waist pouches that comfortably conceal most small and medium frame handguns while still facilitating easy access for you.

The whole purpose of a defensive handgun is to stop the assail-ant, while minimizing the danger to others. In most cases, the num-ber of rounds required to stop one or two assailants at close range will be six or less, so high magazine capacity is not a priority when it comes to a defensive handgun. However, stopping power is impor-tant since a potential assailant may be in close proximity. Small wounds may be insufficient to stop or even slow down an attack, especially if the assailant is within a few feet of you. Generally, you should avoid anything smaller than a .38 caliber, .380 caliber, or 9mm.

Inversely, self-defense combat often occurs in an environment where other, innocent bystanders may be present, so you don't want ammunition that will blast through the target and hit others. The objective is to have all of the energy from the shot expend itself stop-ping and dropping the target only. Even a .45 caliber round will not assure a one-shot-drop. Ammunition that is specifically designed to "mushroom" or fragment on impact provides the most stopping power with the least hazard to others. Self-defense ammunition such as Speer Gold Dot, Hornady Critical Defense™, Winchester Silvertip™, and Winchester Ranger Talon™ are just a few examples. Remember that if you ever need to use this weapon, reliability will be a life-or-death necessity. Don't go cheap on this. Buy a new or used, name-brand handgun from a reliable dealer who can provide a guarantee of quality. Generally flat-stack, automatic handguns are preferable to revolvers for concealability, but there are a few five and six shot revolvers that are fairly small and highly reliable. While you do not need to achieve a high level of accuracy for a weapon that will usually be used at ranges of two to ten feet, you should go to a range and fire at least one hundred rounds to establish its reliability and your confidence. Be sure to clean your handgun after each use according to manufacturer's instructions. In summary, a compact, reliable handgun with six to ten rounds of larger caliber self-defense ammunition should be adequate for most situations.

Combat Weapons

The priorities and requirements for true combat weapons are somewhat different than for urban defense weapons. The term "combat" implies a long-lasting exchange of fire between two or more combatants. Self-defense requires only that you stop the initial crime or assault until escape or the arrival of law enforcement, while combat would imply the need to suppress or terminate hostile forces without the expectation of outside assistance. Here, firepower and accuracy outweigh other considerations. While pitched battles between citizens and gangs of criminals are common in survivalist fiction, most citizens will not need to face such circumstances. A well-armed and prepared individual or family fending off a few looters or intruders is a more likely scenario.

Combat Handguns

Handguns for home defense and open-street combat can be full-sized, heavy-caliber weapons with high capacity magazines. These are kept in handy locations, such as the bedside drawer at home and carried on a belt or vest holsters when evacuating under high-hazard conditions. Accessibility—not concealment—is the key factor. Magazine capacities of seventeen to twenty rounds are desirable and you should have at least four spare, full magazines. Calibers for such weapons are usually at 9mm and above. Nine-millimeter luger, .40

Top row, left to right: Large eight round, three-five-seven-magnum revolver, certainly reliable and powerful, but may be too large for some individuals; small Colt, thirty-eight caliber, six shot revolver, suitable for home defense and even concealed carry, but may be inadequate for a serious gun fight.
Bottom row: Three large auto-pistols with magazine capacities of seventeen to eighteen rounds. The gun on the left has an attached reflex sight and the one in the middle has a combination flashlight and laser beam device attached on the rail below the muzzle.

caliber Smith & Wesson, and .45 ACP are among the most common combat handgun rounds. If the primary use of the weapon is for home defense, then hollow point or frangible ammunition should be kept in the weapon, otherwise load high-velocity, copper-jacketed rounds. Such rounds will travel some distance and penetrate a lot of materials so be aware of what's beyond and behind your targets. This is why a lot of innocent people are killed or injured in the crossfire of large group shootings. I advise you to keep your primary combat handgun and magazines right with your bugout bag as a grab-and-go item.

Combat Shot Guns

For home defense and urban and suburban civil disorder situations, the shotgun has great advantages over handguns and carbines. Just the sight of that big barrel and the sound of a round being jacked into the chamber can be enough to discourage most aggressors. One shot puts multiple projectiles downrange in a pattern that has a much better chance at a first shot hit than any other firearm. A direct hit at close range will positively stop the assailant dead in his or her tracks. A few rounds will send dozens of projectiles downrange, which can stop a large group of attackers. Lower velocity "law enforcement" rounds are ideal for close quarters and indoor encounters since they have reduced recoil and are less likely to injure innocent people further away. With a shotgun, you are firing off about six to ten rounds to the handgun's one or two.

Shotguns also have amazing versatility. You can perforate a vehicle with buckshot or stop it with a slug or armor-piercing round. You can use breaching rounds to open doors or use exploding or incendiary rounds to discourage attackers or clear your escape route. Of course, once you are safe you can still bring down game for food with a shot and slugs. Compared to good handguns and combat rifles, shotguns are relatively cheap. You can get a good, new combat-style pump shotgun for $300 or $400. However, shotguns designed for survival combat such as the Kel-Tech™ KSG with two six-round magazines and a length of just thirty-eight inches can cost up to $1,000. Shotguns are often less regulated than handguns and rifles and attract less attention. You can purchase shotguns with shortened or even folding stocks and there are a variety of accessories available including lights, shell-holders, and laser sight. A 12-gauge shotgun is the standard size and has the most available ammunition types. Long-barreled, hunting shotguns with chokes are not suitable for combat purposes.

This Mossberg Camper™ 12-gauge, pump-action shotgun has been adapted for combat with a pistol-grip, folding stock, and shell holder. Note the various types of ammunition on the folding stock.

Combat and Defensive Long-Guns

You would need a combat-capable long-gun only in the gravest survival situation. In home defense and urban situations, handguns have the advantage of mobility and speed in close quarters; however, if you are forced into defending a building or moving through an urban or rural environment, the range and accuracy of a rifle or carbine designed for defensive combat can be valuable.

In brief, you'll probably want to avoid complex and exotic weapons and calibers. Select a weapon that fires commonly available ammunition such as .223 Remington, 5.6 NATO, 7.62 NATO, or .308 Winchester. If you're buying a rifle in the off chance of a prolonged and intensive combat situation, you need to stock at least 1,000 round or more and have six-to-ten full, thirty-round magazines. Select a rifle based on the popular AR-15 design. There is a wide variety of ling-rifles and carbines that you can purchase and lots of available accessories for them. Be sure to have the necessary manuals, tools, and cleaning supplies. New rifles based on the AR-15 platform range from $700 to over $2,000depending on the manufacturer and design.

There are also some good rifles available based on the famous Russian Kalashnikov AK-47 design. These rifles are extremely reliable,

Top: The AK-47 with a folding stock fires Russian 7.62 millimeter ammunition, extremely rugged and reliable, and ammunition is easily available.
Bottom: The popular AR-15 fires 5.56 NATO ammunition which is typically in plentiful supply, a bit cheaper and less accurate than the versions of the AR-15 that can cost $700 to well over $1,000. I recommend a minimum of three magazines, but having six to eight, thirty-round magazines and several thousand rounds of ammunition is a good investment.

if a bit less accurate than the AR-15-based weapons. These rifles use 7.62 x 39 millimeter Russian ammunition. While this ammunition is commonly available today, it would probably be hard to find under survival conditions, so you would need to stock more in advance. Various surplus and clone versions of the AK-47 are available for $400 to $800. As with all firearms, you should fire them on a safe range and become proficient at firing, changing magazines, and cleaning the weapon. Your selected combat rifle should be kept with your bugout or evacuation bag for quick access.

Other Firearm Options

Scoped hunting rifles are generally unsuitable for combat situations as they are bolt-action, slow-firing, and a bit less mobile in combat. However, they can be valuable in rural or wilderness defense and hunting situations. Scoped versions of the ubiquitous Remington 700 firing .308 Winchester, .30-06 Springfield, .223 Remington, and other calibers are good choices. Light-weight rifles using common .22 Long-rifle-caliber ammunition are important for hunting small game and as a last-resort defense. Break-down models such as the Henry AR-7 and the Chiappa Little Badger™ are lightweight and small enough to fit inside your survival pack. A somewhat larger and more expensive breakdown survival rifle is the TNW Firearms, Aero Survival Rifle™ that weighs six pounds and costs over $500, but has a ten-round magazine and can be converted to shoot .22 Long-rifle ammunition or a variety of pistol caliber rounds. Twenty-two caliber ammunition is small and light enough to carry hundreds of rounds and the report from shooting attracts far less attention than larger calibers.

Slingshots are silent and you can use available small rocks as ammunition. You can use a slingshot to take small game silently or to harass and misdirect an enemy. With some practice you can achieve impressive accuracy. Although they can cause serious injury or even death under some conditions, they are not recommended for self-defense. There are many slingshots specifically designed for survival use.

Left photo: The Henry™ AR-7, .22 caliber survival rifle comes with the bulky, floating stock, but this can be replaced with a compact folding stock purchased online from AR-7 Customized Accessories, LLC. With the barrel detached and the stock folded, the whole gun fits nicely into a pack.

Right photo: This Nomad™ five-piece, take-down bow with two-piece arrows cost about fifty dollars and fits easily into a pack. There are also compact, folding survival bows on the market.

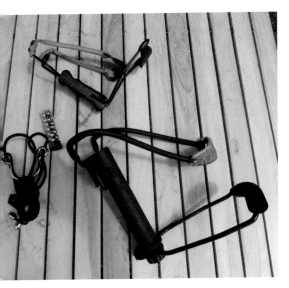

Top row: Wrist Rocket™, light and powerful enough for taking small game.
Bottom row, left to right: Small Trailblazer™ backpack slingshot, costs less than seven dollars and comes with a length of paracord on the handle and an extra set of bands; Large "survival slingshots," sell for as much as fifty dollars. Slingshots are most effective with steel shot (in the clear container), but small rocks and marbles can be used. These sling-shots are from survivalsling-shots.com.

Entry and escape skills and devices can be important in some survival situations.

Top row, left to right: Miniscule 5ive Star Gear Escape Stick™, used to practice escaping from handcuffs; lock picking manual; lock pick gun and bump keys.

Middle row, left to right: An ordinary looking pen that has a handcuff key on the cap, and a selection of lock picks and tension wrenches.

Bottom row: Form of escape stick; Readyman Escape Card™ with saw and lock picks.

Chapter 11
Escape and Evasion Devices

There are many survival and crime scenarios where the capacity to loosen restraints, pick locks, or escape confinement could be essential. You may be cuffed or tied up by aggressors or you may need to open a lock to escape or to access supplies or shelter. The survival market now provides a variety of devices to aid escape. There are training kits and online classes for lock picking. Sets of lock picks, bump keys, and lock pick guns are available for between twenty to fifty dollars. Picking locks and using bump keys requires considerable practice, so having these devices without acquiring some skills is not going to be helpful in an emergency. Small concealable escape tools are only useful if they are truly concealed and are always with you. Your anticipated threats will determine whether you need such devices.

Top row: Non-metallic knife.
Middle row, left to right: Miniature saw and knife; fifty cent coin modified to conceal a rounded razor blade. (These can be used to cut rope, tape, flex cuffs, and bindings.)
Bottom row: Titanium pen with a handcuff key on the cap. Such devices are available from 5ive Star Gear and Readyman.

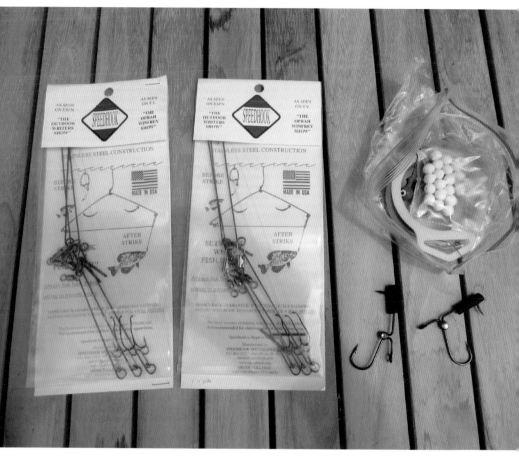

Left to right: Two Speed hook™ three-packs; a small fishing kit; two fishing hooks.

Chapter 12
Fishing and Trapping Equipment

You can usually carry enough survival food for three to ten days, but beyond that you will need to be able to hunt, fish, trap, and forage for additional sources of nourishment. Adding a compact fishing kit and some components for trapping small game to your survival supplies can provide primary or supplemental food found in most regions. Most survival fishing kits include a knife and some sort of pole. While these are handy, a pole can easily be improvised from tree branches and you should already have one or more knives in your survival gear. You need to have about twenty feet of ten-pound test fishing line, some assorted steel hooks, a steel leader, some tin sinkers, and a floating bobber. Most kits include these items.

Fishing kits take up little room in your pack and cost from ten to twenty dollars. The Pocket Reel™ Emergency Fishing Kit is a good choice and can be purchased for less than fifteen dollars. Another option is the Speedhook™ originally made for US Airforce survival kits. This is a set-and-forget, self-activating hook device that can hook fish and small game when they take the bait. The completer unit weighs only a few ounces and cost about ten dollars. A Speedhook™ six-pack that includes six hook sets and bait is just twenty-three dollars. Stealth Angel markets a pocket, portable rod and reel that compacts to just eight inches and expands to a thirty-one-inch rod with a miniature reel attached for just ten dollars. Carrying large and heavy animal traps is not practical, but snares can be effective for small and medium sized game. Such devices are generally not legal or humane, but may be justified in extreme survival situations. Ghost Rider™ is just one brand that offers a variety of cable snares. Of course, snares can be improvised from wire, line, or cable with a little practice.

Chapter 13
Water Storage and Purification

In many survival, disaster, or emergency situations water that is safe to drink will be unavailable. We as a population have become so accustomed to tap and bottled water that it is difficult to comprehend the consequences of water not being readily available. In an urban or suburban environment, a prolonged interruption of water service would quickly result in chaos, looting, and mass evacuation. Alternative sources of water such as rain puddles, streams, and ditches would be heavily contaminated and quickly lead to epidemics. Those who are wise enough to store water and or have the means to purify available water would also be wise to maintain a low profile. People will get desperate from thirst long before they get hungry.

While the general rule for home storage of water is at least one-gallon per person per day, two gallons per day is a better choice. If you have a lot of dehydrated food to reconstitute you may need additional gallons. Because water is so heavy and bulky, its storage potential is limited. A fifty-five gallon drum of water will last a family of three about ten days. There are some good plastic drums with pumps on the disaster preparedness market. At least some of your stored water should be kept in one- or two-gallon containers that can be loaded into your vehicle quickly if necessary. Most municipal water can be stored without additional treatment if the containers

Top row, left to right: Extream-X™ squeeze operated water filter purifies 26 gallons; Katadyn Varo™ pump-operated water filter; canteen with integral water filter.
Bottom row, left to right: Portable Aqua ™ water purification tablets; Super Straw ™ water purifier; Aquatabs™ purification tablets; squeeze-bulb-operated water filter device.

There are all kinds of ways to store water.
Left to right: Two repurposed, bleached food containers; two-gallon camping water container with spout; stackable, interlocking water containers; collapsible one-gallon water jug.

are clean. If you are storing well water or other water you are unsure about, add five to six drops of household bleach to each gallon. Of course you may simply want to buy bottled water at the store. Once your stored water is used up you must have an effective method of gathering and purifying water that you find in rain barrels, ponds, nearby lakes, or streams. While bleach treatment and boiling can be effective, modern water filter and purification systems are the safest and most reliable option. Large home purification systems are an ideal first step towards potential self-reliance.

There are many water carrying and water purification systems designed for the outdoors. One can only carry a few full canteens with an evacuation pack or bugout bag. As you continue your journey, finding sources of safe water to refill these may become difficult. It is essential to have some reliable methods of filtering and purifying whatever water you can find while on the road. Portable purification systems range from canteens with built-in filters, survival straws that can fit in even the smallest survival kit, and compact systems such as the Vario™ microfilter system that can purify hundreds of gallons and has changeable filters. Water purification tablets are cheap and fit into any size survival pack. Since water is so critical, I recommend that you have two methods on hand, such as a pump filtration device in addition to tablets.

There must be fifty ways to start a fire.
Top row, left to right: Ignito™ fire accelerator, Wetfire™ fire accelerator, box of windproof matches.
Bottom row, left to right: Common gas fire starter; torch-style cigarette lighter above a large magnesium spark striker; welders spark striker; two smaller magnesium spark strikers; flint, steel, and char-cloth kit, such as the pioneers used.

Chapter 14
Fire Starters

While starting a fire is often considered an essential survival skill, there are many situations where a fire is not a priority. A fire is primarily used to supply heat or signal for help. Finding or making shelter and staying dry is always more important than building a fire. A large open campfire actually provides little warmth to those standing around it. Whereas a small campfire with a reflector in back and a shelter behind the survivor can be effective.

Fire staring devices are light and small and should be kept in your pockets and in all your survival packs. A flame is always a better starting point than a spark. Windproof, waterproof camp-matches or good Butane lighters are preferable to spark-devices in most cases. Magnesium fire starter sticks come in a wide variety of sizes and prices and should be carried as a backup for starting fires since these devises can be soaking wet and still produce a hot spark to start a fire. You do need to practice catching the spark into a "birds nest" of dry grass or lint and blowing it into a flame. Flint and steel were the main fire-starting tools of the pioneers, but this technique is less efficient than magnesium sticks. Learning to use the flint and steel method can be fun and, if all else is lost, you might find flint or other sparking sources to use in an emergency.

Typical prepackaged survival evacuation pack. These often need to be supplemented to meet the evacuee's specific needs, but are a good starting point towards preparedness.

Chapter 15
Prepackaged Kits and Packs

It is always better to put together your own survival kits, evacuation packs, and bugout bags. When you buy an off-the-shelf pack, you are paying extra for the vendor to select and package each item. The price is usually significantly higher than the sum of the contents. Everyone's survival needs and capabilities will be different, therefore no cookie-cutter, pre-loaded kit is going to be ideal. However, if you are starting from scratch and need to obtain something in a short amount of time, such packs may be a quick fix until you can build your own pack or modify the prepackaged pack to meet your needs.

If you do opt for a prepackaged kit or pack, don't just put it in your closet. You should examine every item and read all the instructions to be ready to quickly access and use them effectively. You'll probably start thinking about items to add or replace as you do this inspection. Periodically check your pack and replace expired or deteriorated items. Typical prepackaged bugout bags contain packaged water, non-perishable food for several days, some form of shelter system, a first aid kit, a flashlight, fire starters, a compass, a whistle, a steel cup or pot, personal hygiene supplies, a mini-stove with fuel, and, usually, instructions. Typical examples are the ReadyWise™ Five-Day Survival Pack at around eighty-five dollars; Legacy Premium, a two-person, bugout bag at $159; and the Stealth Angel, a two-person, seventy-two hour Emergency Kit and Survival Bag at $119. Stealth Angel also offers a Survival Pal™ bag for children at fifty-five dollars. Most available packs are only designed for three to five-days of evacuation survival, but can be supplemented with extra food, water purifiers, and improved shelter to extend usage.

Prepackaged survival kits are small packages of essential items intended to get you through or out of an emergency situation. These kits are handy for use on day hikes, bicycles, motor vehicles, fishing trips, hunting trips, and other outdoor activities. The contents focus on first-aid, signaling, and short-term shelter. There is usually a flashlight, whistle, fire-starter, first aid items, a compass, and some type of Mylar™ survival sleeping bag. Some kits even include flairs. The Ultimate Survival Kit™ from BCB Adventures packaged in a small metal can for sixty-five dollars is typical of this genre. These small field survival kits are commonly available at sporting goods stores.

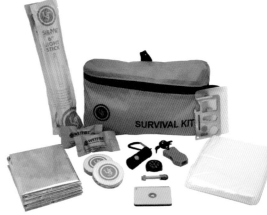

This one-person survival/evacuation kit contains most of what you'll need in an emergency and costs just under $100 from Stealth Angel.

Smaller kits, like this one from Ultimate Survival Technologies, cost less than thirty dollars.

Chapter 16
Books and Training Aids

While the Internet and YouTube are valuable sources for survival-related information and instructions, there is no substitute for books and hands-on training experiences. Electronic media is often subject to failure or inaccessibility precisely when you need it the most. Survival cards and mini-survival manuals are a must for survival kits and packs. A prepared home should have at least basic home survival manuals and first aid books. FEMA and the Red Cross offer some good basic handbooks for the beginner. Military survival manuals are generally not well-suited for home emergency situations. Skyhorse Publishing offers the widest variety of survival-related books, but survival books are included in most survival supply catalogues and websites as well as at sporting goods stores. I have provided a list of recommended survival reading in the appendix of this book. You are of course better off if you actually read these books in advance, before you need the information.

Your choice of books will depend on your anticipated hazards and life style. What you know is always more important than what you have. Don't depend on Google for answers in an emergency.

Left to right: Common garden sprayers can be used for extinguishing class "A" (wood, paper, brush) fires; full-sized ABC dry-chemical extinguisher suitable for dealing with serious fires; smaller ten-pound extinguishers for incipient fires; very small extinguisher suitable for kitchen and vehicle fires. Always have at least two of the large ones available.

Chapter 17
Fire Suppression and Safety Equipment

Fire suppression is often overlooked in emergency preparedness planning. Even during normal, non-disaster times the ability to quickly put out an incipient fire in the home can prevent the total loss of all of your possessions and survival gear, not to mention the occupants' lives. The usual response time for a fire department is five minutes or more. The size of a fire doubles every minute, so a small fire that can be put out with an available extinguisher is likely to seriously damage or destroy your home if unchecked for five or more minutes. During a serious disaster fire, department response time may be delayed or even unavailable. The use of stoves, lanterns, candles, and other potential ignition sources could lead to fires. Criminal activity and civil disorder may include arson. Therefore, having several large, fully charged, ABC[3] class fire extinguishers is an essential part of home safety and home emergency preparedness.

---

3   ABC class extinguishers are rated to put out flammable materials such as wood or paper, flammable liquids such as gasoline or kerosene, and electrical fires.

Having several smoke and carbon monoxide detectors, and changing their batteries every six months, is also essential.

Fire extinguishers can be purchased at most hardware and home supply stores or they can be purchased online from survivalsupplies.com, and other vendors, but you can avoid paying the shipping cost for these heavy items by purchasing from local hardware or safety suppliers. Small one- to three-pound extinguishers that sell for about twenty dollars are handy for your kitchen and vehicle, but I recommend larger, five- and ten-pound extinguishers with a hose, for serious fire suppression. These larger extinguishers sell for fifty to seventy dollars, but are worth every penny. "Almost" putting out a fire is never a good outcome! Every home should have at least three large extinguishers distributed throughout the house. Family members should understand how to use them and if one is in use, another extinguisher should be fetched to use as a backup. If one or two extinguishers fail to put out the fire, everyone must evacuate immediately.

Chapter 18
First Aid Kits, Medical Equipment, and Sanitation

First Aid Kits

Since injuries and medical emergencies are often the source of a survival emergency, or occur as a secondary effect of a disaster, first aid kits must always be part of home survival gear and any type of survival pack. During first aid situations you must assume that either you cannot get to professional medical aid or it will not be available for an extended time, thus such kits must go well beyond basic bandages and salves.

Kit components will depend on the individual's skill levels and anticipated situations. Everyone should know CPR and how to stop severe bleeding quickly. Hemostatic bandages and tourniquet devises such as the TAC™, CAT™, R.A.T.S™, or WAT-T™ should be included with every kit. Large wound compresses and elastic bandages are also important. Most kits will contain tweezers, tape, scissors or EMT shears, nitrile gloves, disinfectants, pain relievers, alcohol swabs, and bandaging materials. Advanced kits often add splinting devices, tourniquets, hemostatic sprays and compresses,

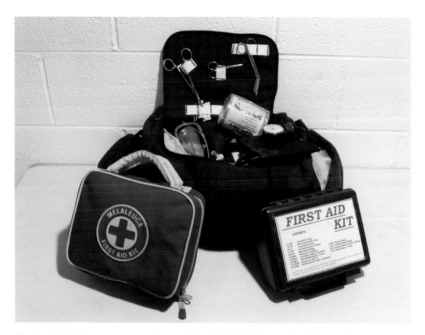

First aid kits can range from the full EMT-grade kit at the center to smaller kits that can be purchased online, at sporting goods stores, or at pharmacies.

triangular bandages for slings, and burn ointment. Kits range in size from small kits sold by the Red Cross such as the Ready™ First Kit at just twenty-two dollars at most sporting goods stores to large para-military backpacks such as the Stomp™ Medical Kit from Live Action Safety at over $300.

ADVANCED MEDICAL CARE EQUIPMENT

Beyond basic first aid kits, there are specialized items that can be used by trained individuals to deal with a variety of serious medical emergencies. Advanced medical and surgical supplies were generally unavailable to non-professionals until the development of the Internet. Today, these items are accessible by all, and instructions and classes are available online and in various traditional classes

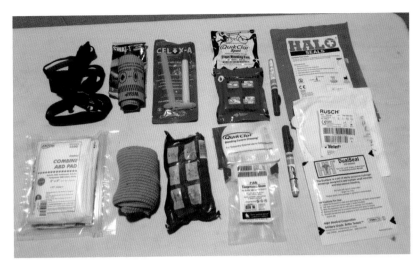

Top row, left to right: Popular CAT™ tourniquet device, SWAT-T™ tourniquet, Celox-A™ hemostatic injector, Quik-Clot™ and Celox hemostatic dressings, ARS™ chest decompression need kit, HALO™ chest puncture seal.

Bottom row, left to right: Sterile wound dressing, Israeli combat wound dressing, US military combat wound dressing, small hemostatic dressings, ARS™ chest decompression need kit, Rusch™, HH DualSeal™ chest puncture seals.

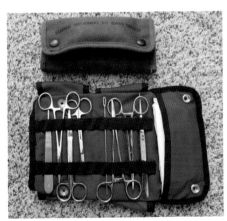

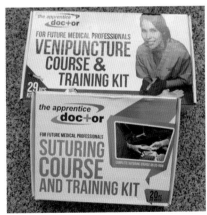

Left photo, Top: Military surplus suture and field surgical kit closed. **Bottom:** Nitro-Pac suture and surgical kit.

Right photo: The Apprentice Doctor offers several self-training medical skill kits including suturing and IV fluids administration.

specifically for laymen. Typical advanced medical items include chest seals for closing sucking chest wounds, needle decompression kits for relieving tension caused by pneumothorax or hemothorax, IV setup kits, airway adjuncts, and suturing kits. The Hyfin™ vented chest seal twin packs sell for about fifteen dollars. TRAK™ needle decompression kits sell for less than ten dollars. Nitro-Pak sells basic suturing kits for thirty-two dollars and full emergency surgical kits for forty-six dollars. They also have larger trauma packs, skin staplers, and airway adjuncts.

Antibiotics for humans are available only by prescription, but antibiotics for animals can be purchased at farm-supply stores right off the shelf. Fish antibiotics such as Cephalexin, Doxycycline, and Amoxicillin are sold at pet supply stores and through survival supply outlets. BUDK sells a bottle of 100, 200, and fifty milligram Cephalexin tablets for about forty dollars, the same size Amoxicillin goes for twenty-five dollars, and Doxycycline at just under sixty dollars. Having a supply of these medications could be critical if access to professional medical care and pharmacies is interrupted after a disaster.

Sanitation

Sanitation is another aspect that is often overlooked when people are preparing for emergencies. Shovels, plastic bags, and plenty of bleach are the minimal requirement for home sanitation. Every survival pack should include a personal hygiene bag containing liquid soap, hand sanitizer, toothpaste and brush, shaving items, and other supplies to stay clean. There are plenty of "travel kits" available in stores. At camping supply stores you can find chemical toilets ranging from just a seat to place on a five-gallon pail at about twenty dollars to more elaborate devices with chemical chambers and seat covers. The Go Anywhere™ portable toilet at seventy dollars is typical for this type. The T-S™ toilet chemical pack is a good investment at just two dollars per package. I recommend keeping plenty of commonly available Wet Ones™ antibacterial wipes in every survival kit

Left to right: High-end chemical toilet, bleach (always have several gallons), shovel, plastic bags, low-cost camper's toilet. Always have lots of TP in stock.

and pack. Larger Bath Pack™ cleansing towels that can provide a full-body cleansing cost only about six dollars and can be a major sanitation, decontamination, and morale boosting item to the bugout bag.

Top row, left to right: Small binoculars, ideal for survival packs and vehicles; large binoculars, more suitable for home use; spare pair of glasses.
Bottom row, left to right: Small binoculars, ideal for survival packs and vehicles; small night-vision monocular, gives you a big advantage in any night survival situation; small monocular, can be carried in the pocket or in small survival kits.

Chapter 19
Optics

Having a spare pair of glasses and a magnifying glass can be life savers in survival situations. This holds especially true for the large segment of the population with pre-existing visual impairments. Even a small monocular or a low-cost pair of ten by twenty-five binoculars gives you a tremendous advantage of being able to see trouble before it gets to you or before you walk into it unawares. On the road, you can identify roadblocks, violence, washouts, and other hazards in advance. At home you can determine if there is a friend or a foe approaching your living space. With good optics you can pick out safe routes, water sources, supplies, game, and usable campsites that might be missed with just the naked eye.

Optics for your pack should be small and durable. Binoculars range from cheap brands that have glued-in lenses to very high-end Zeiss-Terra EDs™ that cost around $500. Tasco binoculars provide satisfactory performance at only thirty dollars, whereas Bushnell are a step up at about one hundred dollars. The Skygenius™ compact binoculars are quite small and can be purchased for just twenty dollars, while a pair of Nikon binoculars can run well over $200. The Hensoldt/Zeiss brand eighty by thirty millimeter German Army Binoculars can be found on the surplus market and provide good value for about $195. Leupols brand offers a high quality ten by forty-two millimeter pair of binoculars for just under one hundred dollars. You have to balance your budget for optics against more essential items, but get what you can reasonably afford without affecting other survival priorities. High-end binoculars can sell for more than $2,000, but are they 200 times better than a pair of one hundred dollar binoculars? Not in my opinion.

Night vision devices were developed late in World War II. Early military surplus equipment was bulky and expensive, but modern night vision scopes, binoculars, and headsets are effective and lightweight. While this gear is intended for hunters and for police SWAT applications, it can be of great value under some survival situations. Many disasters will result in power outages, thus evacuation and escape may necessitate movement through urban or wilderness environments in the pitch dark. While a flashlight may be adequate or even desirable in some cases, the ability to see without being seen may be critical in others. Night vision gives you the advantage of detecting obstacles and threats in your path or identifying potential threats before they reach you.

These types of devices are available in a wide range of designs and prices. Night vision binoculars can cost as little as $150 or as much as $7,000. Reasonably priced sets such as the Stealth Cam™ digital night vision binoculars cost just $170. Head-worn night vision goggles allow the wearer to move through the dark, hands-free, but they are expensive. The cheapest night vision goggles run at around $600, while more advanced sets can run as high as $4,000. Cabela's sporting goods stores offer a variety of night vision devices for hunters. A monocular is a good choice for the survival pack as it is small and relatively light in weight. The Firefield™ night vision monocular costs only about $150 and the Sightmark™ night vision monocular is priced at just under $250. A whole range of night vision goggles, binoculars, and monoculars can be found at Optics Planet, an online store.

Chapter 20

Communications, Monitoring Equipment, and Security

COMMUNICATION AND MONITORING EQUIPMENT

The first rule of survival is to "be aware." Today, that means knowing what is going on in your community and the world. Back in the 1960s when the first small transistor radios came out, they were added to survival packs immediately. Even though they had only AM/FM reception, having a portable method of knowing the weather and what hazards were developing was incredibly useful. Now, we have much more sophisticated radios with a wide range of capabilities that we can use at home or carry in a survival pack.

Small, solar-rechargeable "survival radios" that have AM/FM and weather band reception are available for under fifty dollars. Larger emergency radios that cover AM/FM/WX and GMRS bands with GMRS transmission capability are available for about one hundred dollars. Weather Alert radios that activate automatically to alert you to approaching storms run at about sixty dollars and are sold at local convenience stores. Sets of short-range walkie-talkies that can be set to privacy codes are ideal for emergency communications among nearby family members. Scanners are a must for home and vehicle monitoring of police, fire, and EMS communications.

Purchasing a communication device beyond a basic short wave receiver can keep you abreast of world developments during a truly serious disaster. Acquiring a ham (short wave) radio license puts you in a position to communicate with others regardless of the condition of the commercial radio and phone systems. Midland is one of the most recognized brands of radios designed for the emergency and outdoor market. A set of Midland Xtra Talk™ fifty channel walkie-talkies can be had for about seventy dollars. Such hand-held radios have a range of five to twenty miles depending on conditions. The Midland Base Camp crank AC and battery powered radio with AM/FM/WX and GMRS costs about ninety dollars. A Uniden™ scanner can be had for just under one hundred dollars. Multi-band radios covering AM/FM/GMRS/CB and short wave cost about $140. Good

Left to right: Uniden police, fire, EMS scanner; Midland "Base Camp"™ crank and battery powered AM/FM/WX/GMRS radio with GMRS transmitter; small crank solar powered AM/FM/WX radio that fits into any survival pack; yellow crank and solar powered AM/FM/WX emergency radio; Midland automatic NOAA weather alert radio.

Left: Two commonly available Cobra, twenty-two channel, GMRS, hand-held radios.
Right: BaoFeng™ UHF/VHF FM programmable transceivers. Most GMRS radios are programmable and have security programs to exclude outside listeners. They have a range of up to six miles, depending on location. The UHF/VHF FM radios have greater range, but are more complicated and expensive.

Short wave transceivers and antennas can be expensive and you need an FCC license, but you will have communications under the worst-case scenarios. Basic short wave receivers are more economical and let you listen to the world in an emergency.

short wave transmission equipment and antennas can cost hundreds or even thousands of dollars, but a basic short wave receiver can be had for less than one hundred dollars.

GMRS (General Mobile Radio Service) receivers require a license from the FCC and a fee of seventy dollars. However, CB (citizens band) radios require no license and cost between one hundred dollars and $200. Good short wave transceivers can run from $500 to several thousand dollars depending on their capability, but buying a used transceiver for a few hundred dollars is a practical cost-saving alternative. A "ham" amateur radio license requires the applicant to pass a thirty-five question examination and pay a fifteen dollar examination fee to the FCC. The ability to monitor the major radio frequencies and communicate with family and group members should be a priority to the effective survivalist.

Security and Warning Devices

Home security systems and home video camera monitoring systems are fairly recent developments. The installation of these commercial systems is an option for crime prevention under normal conditions, but may not be operable or effective if the power and the cell towers are disabled. You may also need some sort of warning or intrusion detection device while away from your home or in a survival camp or retreat. During a disaster situation you may be at a greatly increased risk of being a victim of aggressors and looters. It is difficult to maintain a state of constant vigilance since sleep is a survival necessity. Portable security systems fall into three categories: tripwire devices that set off an alarm or flair when an intruder disturbs a wire stretched across a trail, road, or entrance; motion detectors that activate an alarm, send a signal, or take a photograph when someone enters a covered area; and seismic intrusion detectors that send out a signal when the ground is vibrated by footsteps or vehicles.

While there are many ways to improvise trip wire alarms, there are only a few commercial devices available. These are spring-loaded

Top row, left to right: Small infrared intrusion alarm, tripwire activated alarm that activates a light-stick. Similar devices are available that fire a shotgun blank or flair.
Bottom row, left to right: Door wedge alarm and a door handle alarm that set off a loud noise if someone attempts to enter.

systems that fire either a flair or a shotgun shell, or activate a chemical light stick when tripped. You can find these almost exclusively in survival supply outlets. Motion detectors use infrared sensors to detect people or animals moving through a prescribed area. The most common portable version of these systems are motion activated cameras sold in sporting goods stores for hunters to locate game. One example is the Bushnell Nature View™ camera that sells for $140. A lower cost option is the Muddy™ Pro-Cam 14™ at just sixty dollars. These devices have day and night capability and are programmable. High-end models can have wireless connectivity options. Installing seismic intrusion detectors is usually expensive, but you can occasionally find a Vietnam era PSR-1 system with four remote detectors on EBay or from surplus outlets. These units are a bit too big for a survival pack, but are ideal for protecting a camp. They send a signal to the base unit identifying the location of the intrusion, and can be adjusted to ignore small animals.

Another variation of motion sensors are the cheap, battery-powered alarm devices that can be wedged under a door or hung on a doorknob to activate if someone attempts to enter. These are small, practical, and affordable. The SABRE™ Door Handle Alarm just hangs on the inside of the doorknob or another entry point and is set off by any vibration, and you can purchase it for just eleven dollars. The Ideal™ window and door contact alarm senses movement of a door or window being opened. Each unit costs just over five dollars. Door wedge alarms such as the Super Door Stop™ that wedge under a door to stop entry and set off an alarm cost less than nine dollars. Such devices can easily be adapted to field situations and are small enough to carry when traveling with your vehicle or your pack.

Typical trail camera that takes photos of passing wildlife and intruders. More modern versions such as the SpyPoint Link-Micro™ can be synced with your cell phone to provide real-time observation. These devices cost as little as ninety-nine dollars.

Chapter 21
Nuclear, Biological, and Chemical Gear

RADIATION DETECTION EQUIPMENT

Back in the 1960s through the 1980s the "Civil Defense Department" (now FEMA) trained numerous people in radiological monitoring. There were a lot of CD V-742 and 750 dosimeters and CD V-700 survey meters. Additionally, there were complicated nomograms to calculate how long you could be outside. It is important to be aware that detection and monitoring devices are of little value unless you have the knowledge as to how to read them and how to determine safe versus unsafe levels of exposure.

There are a lot of reasonably priced older dosimeters and survey meters on sale at preparedness shows and on the Internet. Uncalibrated radiation detectors sell for about twenty dollars. Since the calibration radiation sources used for this procedure are so strictly regulated, calibrated survey meters sell for about eighty dollars and new detectors sell for about $150. These devices are available from Sportsman's Guide and other survival suppliers. There are also more modern nuclear radiation detectors and monitors on the market.

These range in price from $180 to $300. Regardless of calibration, if you detect any exposure level ranges of area radiation above normal, there is cause for concern and the need to take precautions.

Surplus civil defense survey meters such as the CV-700, 751, 720, etc. can be purchased at preparedness shows and on the Internet at reasonable prices. Some are calibrated and others are not, but calibration services are also available for these. There are plenty of new commercial combination radiation detectors and dosimeters such as the RADEX ONE™ at $125, or the GO GMC300 E PLUS™ at just eighty dollars from Amazon. If you are not limited by budget constraints and you are seriously concerned about a nuclear event, the NukAler™ radiation detector and dosimeter sells for $750.

CD V-742 pocket dosimeters and CD-V750 chargers are also still available from surplus dealers. These are used to register personal exposure rather than area radiation. Dosimeters are intended to be worn in your pocket and checked frequently to determine the

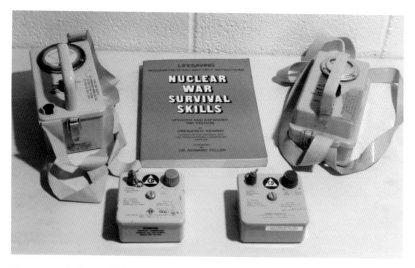

Top row, left to right: Cold War-era radiation detector, best book on nuclear fallout survival, another type of Cold War-era radiation detector.
Bottom row: Two Civil Defense-era chargers for radiation exposure monitors (not shown). Working, calibrated versions of this equipment and special batteries are still available.

amount of radiation to which you have been exposed. They come with a charger and instructions. A charger and two dosimeters sell for about forty dollars. The Survival Shop is a good source for surplus radiation detection equipment. Radmeters4u also offers a full line of new and fully calibrated surplus equipment and will also calibrate instruments sent to them.

Nuclear, Chemical, and Biological Protection Gear

The main objective of NBC (Nuclear, Biological, and Chemical) defense is to keep poison out of your body. Since the respiratory system is the main entry point, respirators are your first line of defense. Fortunately, N95 dust and mist respirators are effective against radioactive dust (fallout) and most biological hazards when used properly.

While the term "N95" generally is used to describe the most common dust and mist masks, it actually refers to the materials used to create the masks and can apply to other types of partial and full-face mask filters. The rating of N95 means that it will filter out at least ninety-five percent of mist and dust particulates based on NIOSH (National Institute for Occupational Safety) "worst case" testing. The "N" indicates that the mask is not oil resistant and will be less effective if exposed to oily mists. The N95 should be adequate for virtually all particulate, soot, mist, and biological hazards. There are respirators rated at N99 and N100, but these are a bit more expensive and will be harder to breathe through. The N95 is not designed to filter out any chemical hazards or gases, but is better than nothing in all cases. N95 respirators with an added layer of charcoal impregnated material offer limited, short-term protection against many chemical agents such as ammonia, chlorine, and hydrogen sulfide, but you must remember that many such chemicals also affect the eyes and skin. If you truly can anticipate exposure to a hazardous chemical gas or vapor, consider this upgrade. Charcoal impregnated masks usually sell for about four dollars each or thirty-five dollars for a box of ten. These are rated as protection against "nuisance chemicals" and are not a substitute for full-face full-filter masks for extended exposures.

Respirators come in variety of styles and options. You can get them with a breathing valve that permits your exhalations to go out through the valve instead of around the face seal. While a rounded mask can be flattened to go into the pocket, you can also buy soft, flat masks that are more convenient to carry. The masks that come with two straps and a pliable metal strip to conform over your nose and mouth fit the best. Masks that have a drinking port are also available for long term use or under high temperature conditions. These are useful for situations where you are using a mask for an extended period of time or in high temperatures where hydration is

Top row: Several military surplus gas masks. If you have these be sure to practice donning them and have extra filters handy. **Bottom row:** Two examples of industrial half-face respirators. These are usually effective against common chemical agents, but should be worn in conjunction with chemical goggles.

essential. These masks should be carried in pockets, in all kits, in all packs, and can be stocked at home as well.

Military surplus and commercial gas masks are intended for prolonged exposure to hazardous chemicals. When your priority as a survivor is short-term escape, N95 masks (changed frequently) should be adequate. I can only justify carrying a bulky gas mask if you anticipate a prolonged exposure to a respiratory hazard. If this is the case there are many reasonably priced options. The Israeli type 80 mask sells for just thirty dollars and the US M-15 mask sells for less than fifty dollars. A Czech M10M mask can be had for just thirteen dollars. These are sold through most survival supply outlets. RDD USA provides a full range of gas masks and escape hoods through their online site.

No filtration mask (even a military mask) will protect you in an IDLH atmosphere. This term refers to a point where the atmosphere is "Immediately Dangerous to Life and Health." When a fire has eaten up all of the oxygen or the oxygen has been depleted or replaced by carbon monoxide, a filter mask will not save you. Burning buildings, pits, tanks, and confined spaces where the oxygen has been depleted or replaced cannot be entered without a full air supply and a breathing apparatus.

NBC Protective Clothing

While emergency responders use elaborate and time-consuming procedures to suit-up prior to working in a nuclear, biological, or chemically contaminated area, the survivor's priorities are much simpler. The first priority is to keep the contaminants out of your lungs using the most immediately available respirator. The second, but also important, priority is to keep the contaminant off of your skin. Fortunately, cheap, lightweight, Tyvek™ suits that are sold at home supply stores are adequate protection from biological agents, radioactive dust (fallout), and most common hazardous chemicals. When you combine these suits with a respirator, goggles, a pair of

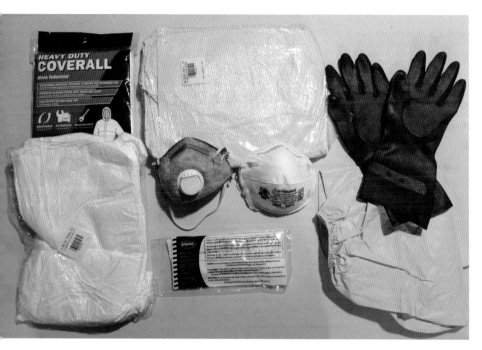

Top row, left to right: Packaged Tyvek coveralls, Heavier TyChem™ coveralls with several N95 respirators, Rubber gloves. **Bottom row, left to right:** unpackaged Tyvek coveralls, TyChem™ boot covers.

rubber gloves, and boot covers you create a good level of protection. Heavier suits such as TyChem™, ChemMax™, or Pro Shield™ offer greater protection but are hot and more expensive. Tyvek™ suits with hoods cost only seven to ten dollars each and have multiple uses in an emergency. In all cases, the survivor must take off the suit, respirator, and gloves immediately after escape from the contaminated area. It is essential to learn the decontamination procedures and undressing procedures in order for you to avoid contact with the contaminated outside of these items. It is important to note that in the absence of protective clothing, any non-porous garment such as a rainsuit or rain poncho can provide some protection.

POTASSIUM IODIDE

Potassium iodide is a specific blocker of thyroid radio-iodine uptake. Consuming potassium iodide effectively prevents the thyroid gland from being saturated with harmful radio-iodide from fallout contamination that can lead to cancer. Fourteen 130 mg potassium iodide pills sell for about twenty dollars from survival supply outlets. The government has stockpiles of these pills for distribution, but having your own supply is highly advisable. Potassium iodide tablets are available through survival supply outlets and at most health food stores and pharmacies at from ten to fifteen dollars a bottle.

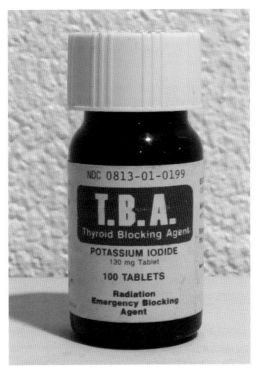

Potassium iodide tablets are available from most survival and preparedness outlets.

Cordage and fasteners are essential for constructing shelter and other applications. Cordage can be purchased at most camping supply outlets. While cordage may be rated for 500 to 600 pounds, it should not be used as climbing rope, since climbing rope is rated for the thousands of pound of strain created by a falling person.

Chapter 22
Cordage

While cordage is often listed as a survival essential, you will only need it for specific situations. The most usual application of cordage is for securing shelters. Cordage can be used to tie together natural materials or secure tarps and tents for shelter. Heavy cordage can come in handy for rescue and escape situations. Military paracord is the most common and useful cordage for survival packs. You can purchase 100 feet of Mil-Spec 550 Paracord for under twenty dollars from Titan Survival and other survival suppliers. Atwood Rope sells fifty feet of sixty-pound test, polypropylene rope for just eight dollars. While rope is not the answer to every survival need, when you need it, you need it. I recommend having at least twenty-five feet of paracord in your pack and having a variety of light and heavier rope and webbing at home that can be handy for many situations.

Top row, left to right: Low cost lensatic compass; Garmen GPS-MAP 64™ model GPS locator, with maps and satellite imagery; Siva™ orienteering compass.

Bottom row, left to right: Durable military lensatic compass with luminous dial; small pin-on compass, handy for pocket or small survival kits.

Chapter 23
Navigation Aids

O ne of the unfortunate effects of modern technology is that few people have retained basic navigation skills alongside the onset of GPS. Map and compass usage was essential to hiking, hunting, and other outdoor activities until recently, and cross-country driving required the traveler to know how to read a basic road map. The introduction of GPS navigation systems for vehicles and smart phones has eroded the public's ability to understand where they are in relation to where they have been and where they are going. People just do what they're told until they "have arrived at your destination." If at any point these systems fail, the average individual will be lost.

We must assume that in any significant emergency, GPS systems will be inoperable and we will need to use pre-GPS navigation methods. Even when you are using GPS systems, I advise you to keep track of the entire route, rather than just the destination, so that you have some idea of where you are and how you got there if the system fails. The old adage "trust, but verify" applies to pretty much any technology that we depend on. While the survivor may carry a modern GPS navigation aid in the survival pack, you must back it up with a good compass and accurate, topographic maps of the anticipated operation area. Up-to-date print-outs of your anticipated routes from Google Earth™ are also useful to include in your evacuation pack. Compasses come in a wide range of designs and prices. A basic lensatic liquid-filled compass can be had for about fifteen dollars and a good military-style compass may cost between twenty and thirty dollars. Most compasses come with glow-in-the-dark numbers, but you can get military compasses with radioactive tritium that glow without prior exposure to light; however, these cost about one hundred dollars. There are all kinds of cheap compasses attached to knives, keychains, and other gadgets that give you a rough idea of your direction. These are BTN (better than nothing) backup devices. A good quality, military-style liquid-filled compass is an essential part of any survival pack. Of course, the device is of marginal use unless you have acquired the basic skills for taking and following bearings, map and compass orientation, and field navigation. Compasses are sold at virtually every sporting goods store, survival gear outlet, and surplus dealership.

Good topographical maps can be acquired from the US Geological Survey website. The site facilitates searching for the exact area you want and the type of map you desire. Topographic map atlases for each state are sold at truck stops and sporting goods stores. These maps are in "one inch equals two-point-five miles" scale and are far more detailed than ordinary road maps. These maps show elevations, rivers and streams, side roads, and other terrain features that could be important under survival conditions. These are also available through the REI website for about twenty dollars. While it is unwise to depend on technology, it can and should be used while it is working. Garmin has pretty much captured the GPS field navigation market. Available Garmin™ hand-held GPS units range from the basic eTrex™ at just $130 to the Rino 750™ that includes a biometric altimeter, NOAA Radio, GMRS radio, and is programmable for around $460. Some of these devices even permit you to ascertain the ownership of the property you are on. These are a great aide to normal camping and hunting, evacuation, training, and route planning.

Chapter 24
Miscellaneous Survival Items

There are a number of items that, while they do not fit into any of the specific categories, *are* worth considering for home preparedness and survival packs.

Smoke Bombs

There are times in an emergency where being very visible is good and other times when being *invisible* is a must. In both cases, smoke bombs can be a real life saver. Carrying a few small colored (red or yellow) smoke bombs in your field survival kit can bring help to you if you are lost or injured. Throwing two or three smoke bombs out to screen an area you must cross or draw attention to a person that must be rescued can keep you from being a visible target. Smoke bombs burn for only a few minutes and you must carefully consider the wind direction, wind velocity, and timing of your throw. How many smoke bombs you have will be dependent on what kinds of situations you anticipate and what areas you may need to get through. Yellow and orange smoke is the most effective for screening as well as for getting attention. White smoke is better if you need to create a diversion or smoke screen without attracting too much attention.

You can get fused multi-colored smoke bombs at fireworks stores for about two dollars each. These are fairly effective, but the paintball game business has made a variety of better smoke "grenades" in all kinds of colors that are ignited by pulling on a ring. Smoke grenades range from 25,000 cubic feet of smoke for under ten dollars each to 70,000 cubic feet of smoke for under twenty dollars. They now make "cool burning" grenades in the same price ranges. I would advise using these in urban and wooded areas. In addition to paintball supply stores and fireworks stands, there are lots of commercial sources online that offer smoke bombs for sale.

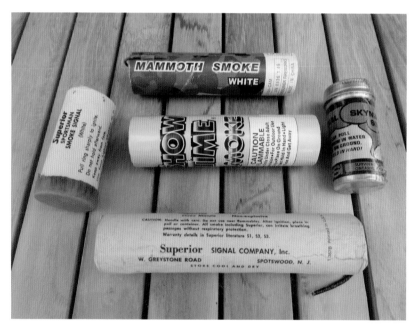

Smoke bombs come in a variety of sizes and types; some have fuses that must be lit, while others have pull-tabs that light them.

FLAIRS

Having a few flairs or a flair gun may be a wise addition to your survival gear since you may need to be rescued at some point. Emergency flairs

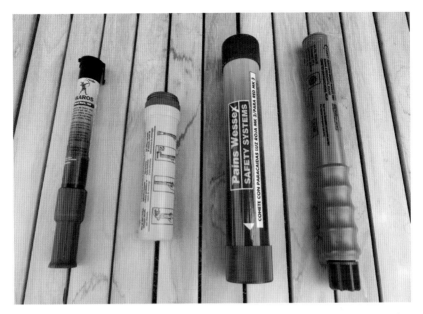

Examples of handheld flairs and parachute flairs which are available from boating supply outlets.

can be purchased at boating supply stores or online. West Marine sells a four pack of handheld flairs for just thirty-five dollars, a four-pack of SkyBlazer™ aerial flairs for eighty dollars, and a 25-milimeter flair gun for $165. The Orion™ twelve-gauge flair pistol with four flairs is a good value at just eighty dollars.

Mini-Books and Survival Cards

No one can remember everything that you could need to know under every survival situation, but you can carry some information with you. Even the most knowledgeable survival practitioner needs a memory jogger now and then. Camping stores, survival supply outlets, and online sources like eBay and Amazon often carry various types of survival information cards and small survival manuals that can fit into your pack. The Sea and Sky™ wilderness survival playing

Top row, left to right: US Army Rangers Handbook SH-21-76, Vietnam-era Survival Cards for Southeast Asia, US ARMY Soldiers Handbook for survival in cold weather.

Middle row, left to right: SAS Survival Guide published by Collins Gems; Pocket Partner policeman's handbook published by Sequoia Publishing, Inc.; Emergency/Survival Handbook from the American Outdoor Safety League, includes a reflective center page to use as a signal mirror.

Bottom row, left to right: Edible plant identification cards from Wild foods, Inc.; survival bandana imprinted with survival information from 5ive Star Gear; set of plastic coated survival cards. Some of these items are out of print, but are still available through eBay and Amazon.

cards cover forty-two categories of survival information for less than eight dollars. You can get a set of Urban Survival Cards from urban-survivalguide.com for seventeen dollars, and Trailblazer™ survival playing cards from Cutlery USA for around eleven dollars. Of course, there are plenty of survival information apps available including the SAS Survival Guide (pictured on previous page), the American Red Cross first aid guide, and the Bugout Bag Checklist. Depending on these in a serious disaster emergency may seem counterintuitive, but they are useful tools that can come in handy when you are in a bind.

ESSENTIAL KITS

In survival situations, little things can mean a lot. Here are few small, low cost kits that can be purchased at a drugstore that you will want to include in your survival pack.

- **Toothache kits** include medication to alleviate pain and items to temporarily fill a cavity. I advise you to maintain good dental health to prevent needing this kit, but Murphy's Law could make a painful appearance at the worst time.
- **Denture repair kits** are essential if you have dentures. Not being able to eat is a serious survival issue.

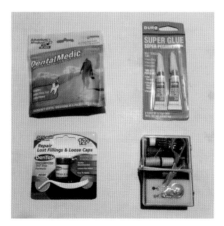

Top row, left to right: Dental repair kit; super glue, handy for many repairs and can be used to close wounds. **Bottom row, left to right:** Toothache kit (if you wear dentures, there are repair kits for them too); sewing kit for clothing, tents, etc.

- **Glasses repair kits** are a good addition if you normally wear glasses, as is a spare pair of glasses.
- **Sewing kits** are useful because clothing can get torn under rough, survival conditions, and you aren't likely to find a tailor or a clothing store after a major disaster.

INSECT REPELLENT AND INSECT SCREENING

Wilderness areas are teaming with insects that carry a variety of diseases. During a serious breakdown of sanitation systems the insect populations of urban areas would explode, spreading life-threatening pathogens. Having a good supply of insect spray at home and small pump-applicators or spray-applicators in your survival pack would help you stay safe. Repellents containing DEET™ are effective against mosquitos, biting flies, ticks, chiggers, and gnats. Good insect repellent can be purchased at your local pharmacy. If you anticipate camping in an insect infested area, you may want to carry

In some regions, insects can be a serious health problem. Always include a small bottle of insect repellent in survival packs and consider mosquito netting in some areas.

mosquito netting in your survival pack. A thirty-two by seventy-eight foot net costs about fifteen dollars at outdoor sports stores and surplus outlets.

INFLATABLE RUBBER BOATS

If you live in a floodplain or you anticipate the need to evacuate down or across a river, you may want to consider including an inflatable rubber boat in your preparedness gear. They are too heavy for the pack, but can be placed in your vehicle or kept at home. I have observed people using them to carry out their valuables from a flooded home, or self-rescue themselves and their families. Spreetail™ sells a large rubber boat for $239. Smaller two- and four-man rubber boats can be found at surplus outlets and sporting goods stores for under one hundred dollars.

This Saturn Budget inflatable boat is available from boatstogo.com for $495, and is perfect for flood survival and evacuation by water situations. This type of boat is usually available at sporting goods stores.

I recommend good quality, rubberized tote bins and steel ammunition cans for storage of all your emergency survival gear. Tote #33 contains my survival pack, boots, and other "ready to go" items. Other totes contain food, medical supplies, and protective clothing. The ammo cans on the right contain communications equipment and, of course, ammo.

Chapter 25
Storage and Maintenance

Since most survival and emergency preparedness items will be stored for long periods of time, but must be in good condition immediately when needed, safe and secure storage is essential. Storing your survival gear in cardboard boxes, wooden crates, or plastic bags is not acceptable. The major threat to your survival gear is moisture in the form of damp air. Other hazards include floods, fires, and theft. All critical survival equipment, including survival packs, food, and medical supplies should be kept in high quality rubberized tote bins with secure covers. Avoid cheap plastic tote bins that can crack and leak. Military surplus ammunition containers are ideal for storing food, ammunition, electronics, medical supplies, and other critical gear.

Stored metal items should be lightly oiled and wrapped in plastic wrap. Since you may need to move your equipment quickly in an emergency, all containers should weigh less than thirty pounds each when filled. Be able to move it or be prepared to lose it. Whenever it is practical, store survival equipment high enough to avoid it being contacted by seepage or flooding. Keep it high and keep it dry. Try the older steel and newer plastic surplus fifty-caliber ammunition cans which cost between fifteen and twenty-five dollars from Sportsman's Guide or at gun shows and surplus dealers. It's a good idea to place silica-gel, desiccant packs in containers with moisture sensitive (rot and rust) equipment to keep these items dry. One hundred small one-gram packs cost about eight dollars. Two online sources for silica-gel packs are Widgetco and Uline.

Firearms, electronics, and other items will have maintenance and storage instruction on the labels. Since their ability to function could be critical to surviving, you should read and heed every word. All survival gear and supplies should be inspected at least twice each year. Deteriorated or out-of-date items should be replaced as needed. Assuming that the stuff you put away ten years ago will be in tip-top shape when you need it most is not good thinking.

If you have a detached shed or garage, consider storing some of your gear or backup gear there. If anything happens to one building, you may still be able to save some of what you need in the other location.

Chapter 26
Survival On a Budget

Most survival fiction involves a hero with an unlimited budget, who is equipped with the latest and most expensive gear. Some survival and preparedness books seem to be written by salesmen, promoting brand names and only high-end products. Establishing such high standards and limited choices is a disservice to the average citizen who has to balance emergency preparedness needs against paying for the necessities of everyday life. While it would be ideal to go out and buy everything a person or a family would need to meet every conceivable emergency, such an approach is financially impractical for most of us. After over fifty years of preparedness, I still do not have everything that I could possibly need for every conceivable emergency. There is an old Chinese proverb that goes, "The best time to plant a plum tree is twenty years ago, the second best time is today." In other words: start now, do as much as you can, and constantly improve your level of preparedness. The following are a few questions to consider as you make your purchases.

- Will this item be used constantly or just be needed for an emergency? If you will be using the item for camping, hunting, or other activities on a regular basis, then its toughness and resistance to long-term wear-and-tear are more of a factor.

- How much can I afford to spend on this item without sacrificing funds needed for other survival needs? For example, spending too much on firearms and ammunition and not leaving enough for adequate food, shelter, and medical supplies would not be balanced thinking.
- Am I paying for higher quality or just for a brand name? Does a $400 knife cut eight times better than a fifty dollar knife?
- What can I afford to buy to cover a survival necessity now until I can upgrade? Remember that anything that works is BTN (better than nothing).
- Are there surplus or used items on the market that can cover this survival need? Military surplus items are often of higher quality than commercial items.
- Is this item likely to be lost or broken? If it's likely to be lost or broken, you may want to have two or more medium-priced items instead of one high-priced one.
- Can I improvise with household items until I can afford to buy purpose-built products? For example, there are lots of dried, long-shelf-life foods in the grocery stores that can be used in place of freeze-dried products. Many kinds of luggage have straps that can double as your survival pack.

A balanced program that prioritizes the most essential survival needs such as water, food, shelter, first aid, etc., based on your anticipated survival needs is essential. A reasonable and organized budget aimed at (1) covering all your needs, and (2) consistently improving the quality and quantity of your gear and supplies is the key.

Chapter 27
Putting It All Together

Having what you need, where you need it, and when you need it is the key to surviving most emergencies and disasters. "Have what you need" is one of my principles of survival. Another one of my survival mantras is, "It's not what you have, it's what you have with you that counts." Having a lot of "survival stuff" is not good enough, the stuff must be well-selected and organized to meet your anticipated survival situations and needs. Most people are at home about sixty percent of the time, so building up what you need to survive a "shelter in place" situation is a first priority. But we may be at our place of employment or on the road when a disaster develops, so having small "get home" kits at work and in your vehicle is also important. Ultimately, we may be forced to evacuate from our community or even retreat and survive on our own for prolonged periods, depending on our skills, planning, and what items we can carry in a backpack. There is no such thing as a perfect, one-size-fits-all survival kit or pack. Every individual's environment and range of potential needs may be different, but the foundation needs of safe air, clean water, adequate nourishment, sufficient shelter, necessary medical aid, and effective self-protection must be included every time.

Home Preparedness

In most cases you will either be home or go to your home in the early stages of a developing emergency. The situation may resolve within a few days, or extend into weeks or even months. Stocking up and staying in is usually preferable to packing up and taking off. You should put effective and comprehensive home preparedness as the first step towards survival and self-reliance. Basically, you must have enough of anything that you might need to last you a few weeks or longer without going outside at all.

You should start by storing as much water as you can in one or two gallon containers and purchase a large capacity water purification device. I also advise keeping at least five gallons of bleach available for water purification and sanitation. You are not limited to expensive, freeze-dried foods for home survival; you can use off the shelf grocery store canned goods, and nonperishable staples like pasta, beans, and nuts to stock your survival pantry. You'll want a camp stove and plenty of fuel for cooking and probably camp heaters as well. While you may have plenty of blankets, you should consider getting sleeping bags if you live in a colder climate. Solar charging lanterns and flashlights and a solar charger panel are a must.

Since disasters often result in injuries or illness you should have a good stock of first aid items and, if possible, prescription medications and antibiotics. Your toilet may not work and the garbage may not be picked up for weeks, so a camp toilet, bleach, shovel, and lots of trash bags are essential. Stock up on toilet paper too. Of course, all of your shelter-in-place preparations depend on your ability to have a place. If you are driven from your home by looters, or your home is damaged or burned down all is lost, so fire extinguishers, firearms, and repair tools are also key elements in your preparations. Portability is not a major factor in home preparedness, so weight and space are less important than stockpiling items that will enhance your long-term survivability and self-reliance.

Get Home Packs

You may be caught in the beginning of a terrorist attack, an epi-demic, large-scale natural disaster, or general civil disorder while you are many miles from home. Having the pocket items described in Chapter 2 will certainly give you an advantage, but having a special-ized kit or pack that will keep you alive and safe as you work to get home can improve your chances immensely. Get home packs are not full evacuation packs or survival packs, as they must be small enough to have with you at all times, yet they should contain the items you will need to travel and survive over a distance. You are not going to go around wearing your get home pack under normal conditions, so it needs to fit into your desk drawer, vehicle trunk, locker, or other accessible locations.

You need to consider what the most likely scenarios are and how far and how long you will need to travel, as well as through what environments when you are selecting your pack's contents. If your pack is intended to get you home from your job, school, or other familiar locations you may already know the routes and may not need to carry maps and a compass, but if you travel to varied and distant locations, you will certainly need to include good maps, a compass, and a GPS device. The average person walks at four miles-per-hour, but disaster situations may involve obstacle and detours, so as little as twenty miles-per-day may be anticipated. The get home pack is intended to get you home within one or two days through dangerous and possibly hostile conditions, so it is necessarily heavy on first aid, respiratory protection, and self-defenses while being lighter on food, water, and other long-term needs.

Get Home Pack Items

1. Two or more N95 respirators: Terrorist attacks, chemical incidents, fires, and many other situations will result in an unsafe atmosphere.

2. A plastic rain poncho: This item will protect you from airborne contaminants, rain, and wind.

3. A first aid kit: Many types of emergencies will result in injuries. Basic bandages, a tourniquet, pain relievers, antiseptic ointment, and hemostatic gauze pads should be included.

4. Self-defense weapons: Disaster situations can result in civil disorder and looting. If at all possible include a small handgun and extra magazines of ammunition in your kit. If this is not an option, include a large can of pepper spray and possibly a Taser. Better to have it and not need it than need it and not have it.

5. A good pocket knife or multi-tool: These have many critical applications during a survival situation.

6. A small AM/FM/WX band radio: Knowledge of developing situations will be critical to your reaching home safely.

7. A small monocular or binoculars: Seeing hazards and checking route safety in advance will be an important advantage.

8. A hand-held GMRS walkie-talkie: If you have established a plan with your family, this could be used to communicate with them as you get close to your home.

9. A tactical flashlight: Disasters frequently result in power outages. You may need to move through darkened areas at night or signal for help.

10. A loud whistle: This is always handy for signaling for help.

11. Several days' worth of your prescription medications: You can never be sure how long before you can get more.

12. One or two pints of water: Water may be not be critical during short-term escapes, but you should still carry some. Adding a few water purification tablets or a Survival Straw™ may be a good idea, just in case.

13. A lighter, matches, or magnesium stick: Starting a fire may not be a priority, but it's better to have the ability if needed.

14. Short-term, energy food: While you don't need to have cooking gear and meals, you do need fast energy and nourishment.

Top row, left to right: Military-style "assault pack," innocuous backpack.
Bottom: Large fanny pack.

The contents of a Get Home Pack depend on your anticipated distance, route, and hazards, but should be heavy on first aid, self-rescue, and self-protection items regardless.

123

Energy bars, protein bars, and trail snacks for two or three days along with caffeinated five-hour energy drinks are a must.

15. Navigation aids: Maps, compasses, and GPS devices are only necessary if you are unfamiliar with the routes to your home.

EVACUATION PACKS

Most emergency management agencies advocate having an evacuation pack ready. As the name implies, these packs are designed for short-term evacuation from your home to a designated shelter or camp where you will be provided with food, medical care, and shelter. Most localized short-term disasters resolve within a few days, so these packs should have just enough basic items to get you through a few days on the road. Of course, the contents can also be used to aid in a shelter-in-place situation. The Red Cross and other agencies actually sell pre-packaged evacuation kits to the public. Having a basic evacuation kit for every family member is the absolute minimum preparedness level for any responsible family today.

The list below is a modified version of the FEMA seventy-two-hour Evacuation Pack list. These items are enough for one person to get through a few days of travel to safety. Each family member should have one. Children can have smaller bags as well. In most cases evacuation is a last resort, but the items in the pack can be used for home emergencies as well. These items can be kept in a small backpack or carry-on type bag.

1. Four sixteen-ounce water bottles: These can be replaced by one or two canteens and should be supplemented with a package of water purification tablets.
2. One collapsible stove with heat tablets: The folding Esbit stove is ideal for this application.
3. One metal canteen cup or Sierra™ cup: Being able to prepare hot drinks is important for maintaining energy and morale.

4. One fifty hour-candle: This can be substituted with a solar rechargeable mini-lantern.

5. One tactical flashlight: Consider one that has multiple power levels or is solar rechargeable.

6. One multi-band radio: This should be AM/FM/WX weather band, preferably crank and solar powered.

7. One to four food bars: High calorie, high protein food bars and trail foods that have long storage-life. Consider life-boat rations that provide 2,500 calories.

8. One large rain poncho.

9. Two N95 dust and mist respirators: These provide protection from airborne contaminants, but also help retain respirator warmth.

10. One space blanket: While cheap rescue blankets are lighter, the much more durable Space Blankets™ provide better shelter and warmth.

11. One multi-function knife: A Swiss Army type knife or a multi-tool will come in handy for many purposes.

12. One box of waterproof matches: You may want to add a lighter or a magnesium spark striker to be sure you get a fire.

13. One bottle of hand sanitizer: An alcohol-based sanitizer can serve as an aid to fire starting as well as to keep your hands clean.

14. One first aid kit: Include bandages, hemostatic gauze pads, antiseptic, and pain relievers.

15. One pair of extra glasses: If you normally need glasses this is a must.

16. One spare pair of heavy socks: If you will be walking a long distance extra socks are important. Sore, wet feet can stop you in your tracks. Socks can also serve as mittens in cold weather.

17. Extra prescription medications: Take as much as you can since you cannot depend on a resupply in an evacuation.

18. Six light sticks: FEMA recommends these and they could be useful when navigating at night.

Top photo, left to right: Heavy-duty, military-style assault pack, ideally suited for use as an evacuation pack, but any good small pack will suffice; Small pack, will attract less attention.

Middle photo: All of the listed contents of a good evacuation pack.

Top row, right: While the four bottles of water are recommended by FEMA, I prefer one or two plastic canteens or stronger water bottles since they are less likely to leak and can be used to purify water using Aqua Tabs™.

Middle row, left: Alternatives to the red Space Blanket™ are the Mylar™ survival blanket and the green Titan brand emergency sleeping bag on top of it.

Bottom row, left: Two examples of N95 respirators next to a folded Tyvek™ suit for protection from contaminants.

Bottom photo: A few examples of light-weight, non-perishable foods suitable for any kind of survival kit or pack. The coffee and tea bags in the lower left corner and the oatmeal packets in the middle require the use of a metal cup and a stove or fire. If you include these, don't forget a spoon or a knife, fork, and spoon combination like the one shown.

19. Paper copies of vital documents: Birth certificates, deeds, mortgages, titles, and insurance papers. Also include your medical and contact information.

20. Self-protection device (optional but recommended): Under some conditions you may be subject to criminal assault and looting. Options range from pepper spray to a handgun. Be aware that government shelters probably will prohibit and confiscate weapons.

21. Optional food: Your stove can be used to heat up coffee, tea, instant soups, and other beverages, so consider adding instant coffee, tea bags, sugar packets, and bouillon cubes to your pack. If you include oatmeal or thick soups, don't forget a spoon.

Outdoor Survival Kits

Outdoor survival kits are intended for coping with unexpected, short-duration outdoor emergencies such as being caught in a storm, getting lost, or being injured. The content of the kit depends on your outdoor activities. A kit intended for a day-hike would be different than one for a hunter or a mountaineer. The outdoorsman usually carries a canteen of water and a knife, and will be adequately clothed for the environment, so these are usually not part of the kit. Rescue is a primary issue here so you should include a cell phone, flairs, smoke bombs, signal mirrors, and whistles. Fire starting matches and magnesium sticks, and energy bars or jerky provide sources of warmth and sustenance. Staying dry is a primary survival need, so a good rain poncho is an indispensable item. If you don't carry a compass normally, then one should be in this pack. A few basic first aid items and pain medication should also be included. There are many versions of Mylar™ survival sleeping bags and blankets that are light, small, and fairly effective in preserving body heat, so one of these should be in your outdoor survival kit. A pair of heavy socks is a good addition to any outdoor kit, since they can replace wet socks or be used as mittens in an emergency. Always inform others of your intended route and anticipated return time before venturing into the outdoors. Your survival kit is intended to sustain you for a few days and aid in your rescue, but if no one knows you are missing or where to search for you, these items may not be enough.

1. Water and water purification methods: Depending on the climate, you should always carry a quart or two of water with water purification tablets or a Survival Straw™ as a backup.
2. Fire starter: You should have at least two methods of starting a fire such as a lighter and a magnesium striker.

The contents of an outdoor survival kit will be heavy on shelter, warmth, signaling, and water.
Top row, left to right: Water filtering canteen, package of Aqua-Tabs™, Survival Straw™.
Bottom row, right: The compass on top of the orange rain poncho is an essential for any outdoor adventure.
Background: Large fanny pack, ideal for carrying a survival kit.

3. Shelter and warmth: Depending on the size of your kit this can be a small Mylar™ Survival Blanket or Survival Sleeping Bag, or a bit larger Emergency Sleeping Bag or Space Blanket.

4. Signaling devices: Whistles, signal mirrors, flairs, and smoke bombs are essential to summon help.

5. Extra socks: A spare pair of socks can replace cold wet socks or lost mittens in cold conditions.

6. Rain poncho: A major rule of survival is "never get wet."

7. Wool cap: The weather can change quickly. A wool cap can significantly improve your body warmth.

8. A small flashlight: This will be essential for moving at night and for attracting attention.

9. First aid items: A few bandages, hemostatic pads, and a tourniquet should be included in your outdoor survival kit.

10. Medications: Always carry several days' worth of your prescription medications along with some pain relievers.

11. A compass and maps: If you have these with you, you should be able to avoid getting lost.

12. Short-term nourishment: Include some trail-mix, energy bars, or other non-perishable foods.

13. A knife or multi-tool: If you are outdoors, you should already be carrying one of these, but if not then add it to your kit.

14. A weapon: If you can anticipate any kind of animal or human threat while in the wilderness, then carry an appropriate weapon. Pepper spray may be adequate. Of course, if you're hunting or just normally carry a firearm in the outdoors you will have this covered.

VEHICLE SURVIVAL KITS

The majority of the population spends anywhere from several hours to over a quarter of their hours per week in personal transportation vehicles. Vehicles and their occupants are highly vulnerable to a variety of emergencies. Storms, blizzards, floods, earthquakes, civil disorder, and other events can leave you stranded or trapped in a vehicle for days. Mass disasters can result in thousands of stalled, wrecked, and trapped vehicles, while cell phone services are down and emergency services are overwhelmed. Driving through rural areas can result in you becoming lost or careening off the road when no one is looking for you. In such events, you may be on your own for several days before help arrives.

While vehicles provide shelter from rain and wind, they radiate heat which makes them into freezers in the winter, so blankets, survival bags, and warm drinks become a priority. Methods for signaling for help and marking your location such as flairs, flashers, and flashlights are a must. While food is generally not a priority for short-term survival, it does help to maintain morale, and could be important for extended situations. Vehicle support items such as tow chains, jumper cables, and emergency starter units may be a good investment. In colder climates shovels, cat litter, and carpet sections may help to get your vehicle out of snow drifts. Accidents often result in injuries, so a first aid kit is essential. Last but not least, always have a fire extinguisher in your vehicle, as this can mean the difference between only damage and a total loss of your vehicle. While many of the items listed are essential, some depend on what kind of weather and road conditions you anticipate.

1. Water: Four to six sixteen-ounce bottles of water should be carried in each vehicle at all times.
2. A high-quality, high-powered flashlight: Some models include multi-colored flashing lights for emergencies.
3. Road flairs and reflectors: These can be placed so as to prevent you from being struck by other vehicles.
4. A can of Fix-A-Flat™ tire inflator and sealer.
5. A basic first aid kit: These are available at most auto supply stores and pharmacies.
6. Cat litter or sand: This can be essential to get out of ice and snow.

Top row, left: The large power-pack is optional.
Middle row, right: The heavy come-along device is optional. If you have room, you can replace the small Mylar™ blankets and the red Space Blanket™ with a real wool blanket.

7. A shovel or folding shovel: Useful for digging out of snow and mud.
8. A tow rope or chain: This will help others pull you out of ditches and snow drifts. You may opt for a block-and-tackle or a come-along device that you can use to pull your vehicle out even without help.
9. A set of jumper cables: This helps you get started if your battery goes dead. Better yet is to carry a fully charged portable power-pack.
10. A fire extinguisher: Most automotive fires can be quickly extinguished, but if you don't have an extinguisher all is lost.
11. A blanket: This can be a true wool blanket, a Mylar™ rescue blanket or a Mylar™ sleeping bag depending on the space available in your vehicle.

12. Non-perishable food bars: A few energy-bars and caffeinated stay-awake drinks often found at gas stations and convenience stores will help you get through most situations.
13. Ten or twelve tea candles: These should be wrapped in aluminum foil and kept with some matches. Place the foil on the dashboard and place one or two candles on it. The lighted candles can significantly warm the passenger compartment. You can even warm beverages over them.
14. Work gloves: Needed for warmth and work.
15. Hand wipes and rags: For cleaning hands and equipment.
16. Rain Poncho: Rain and wind protection in case you have to walk to get help.
17. A knife or multi-tool: Always needed for various repairs and improvisations.

LONG TERM SURVIVAL (BUGOUT) PACKS

Survival packs, often referred to as "bugout bags" are generally considered the ultimate expression of self-reliance. Unlike survival kits and evacuation packs, the survival pack is based on the assumption that (1) no help will be forthcoming, and (2) that the disaster situation may be for an extended or indefinite duration. The major weight and space increases as opposed to other types of packs results from the requirements below.

- The survival pack should have sufficient food and water purification capacity to last at least six to ten days.
- The survival pack should have adequate sheltering and warmth items for extended outdoor survival in cold and wet conditions.
- The survival pack should have tools necessary for self-reliance and survival beyond ten days, such as shovels, axes, fishing gear, game traps, firearms, ammunition, etc.

- The survival pack should have enough medications and first-aid items to maintain your health without outside help for extended periods.

While the true survival pack must have more of these heavier and bulkier items, it also must be carried for longer distances, so the selection of items and the pack itself require considerable thought. The rule for putting together a survival pack is to have as much as you are able to carry for five miles between rest stops. You must carefully consider your physical condition, age, and the terrain you will be moving through. Experienced backpackers can carry a lot more than the average citizen, who may not carry the pack until they are forced into a survival situation. Most inexperienced people tend to overestimate how much they can comfortably carry. In creating a survival pack, weight and space is everything! Go for the best, the lightest, and the smallest to make room for food, shelter, and other true essentials. Be draconian in discarding items that you may want, but don't need. The specific contents and amounts of each item will depend on your anticipated needs, budget, and carrying capacity.

STUFF KEPT WITH THE PACK THAT GOES ON THE BELT OR INTO YOUR POCKETS

There are many items that you can store with your survival packs, but can be carried outside of the pack when the emergency occurs.

1. Field boots for hiking: If you need your pack, chances are you should not be wearing sneakers or flip-flops where you are going.
2. Cap or weather appropriate hat.
3. Some energy bars, trail mix, or jerky for the pockets.
4. A full quart canteen and pouch to carry it.

5. A field knife: One such as the Marine Ka-Bar, US Air force Survival Knife, or Smith & Wesson brand Search & Rescue™ knife. If your knife does not have a sharpening stone on the sheath, be sure to have a sharpening stone or sharpening device in your pack.

6. Sunglasses.

7. A weapon: Pepper spray works if all other options are unavailable. I recommend a good handgun, such as a Beretta, Glock 9mm, or Colt .45 caliber auto pistol with holster and extra magazines where legal.

8. A long gun: Depending on your situation, you may elect to carry a more elaborate weapon. This could be a shotgun, rifle, or carbine. You will probably need to carry extra magazines of ammunition in your pockets or bandoliers. Ammunition is heavy and will need to be balanced against food, water, and other critical supplies that you will need to carry.

A complete Bugout pack with associated gear, including boots, a handgun with multiple loaded magazines, a holster, and a suitable long gun.

Bugout Pack Contents

Outer Compartments

1. Water purification device: Katadyn Hiker™, Extreme™, etc. works well.
2. Magnesium fire starter: I recommend the Gerber Strike Force™ or something similar.
3. Compact, folding camp shovel.
4. Miniature solar and crank powered radio: You will want one with AM/FM/WX weather band.
5. Miniature survival guide book or survival information cards.
6. Two large smoke bombs.
7. Twenty-five feet of strong cordage.
8. Lensatic compass and (optional) GPS navigation device.
9. Several energy bars and trail snacks.
10. Large hemostatic gauze pad (Celox™ or other).
11. Spare prescription glasses.
12. Small binoculars or monocular.
13. Multi-tool (e.g. Swiss Army Knife, Gerber, etc.).
14. Tactical flashlight.
15. Prescription medications (reserve supply).
16. Water purification tablets.
17. Waterproof matches.
18. Two N95 dust and mist respirators.
19. Document Package: Include copies of your birth certificate, insurance papers, property titles, will, medical information, critical phone numbers, etc.
20. Emergency plans and maps of routes and safe areas.
21. Small roll of electrical tape.
22. Notebook and pencil.

Main Compartments

1. Heavy-duty Rain Poncho (on top for quick access).
2. Heavy-duty Space Blanket™ aluminized with grommets.
3. Insulated blanket or light sleeping bag tied to outside of pack.
4. Tub tent or twelve foot by twelve foot, three millimeter plastic tarp.
5. Lg. Tyvek™ chemical protective coveralls with attached hood.
6. Wool watch cap.
7. Two pairs of warm socks.
8. Two Chemical light sticks or UV Paqlite™ sheets hung outside pack to charge during the day.
9. One small towel.
10. One roll of twelve inch by twenty-four inch HD aluminum foil.
11. One cooking kit, which should include one small pan and one deep pot.
12. One folding stove MRE Pocket Rocket™, or Esbit™ stove.
13. Two 3.6 ounce gas fuel cylinders for your stove or a box of Esbit™ fuel cubes.
14. One package of fire starter magnesium bars.
15. One knife, fork, and spoon set.
16. Six to eight Mountain House™ freeze-dried meals.
17. Six to eight packages of instant oatmeal.
18. One can of Spam™ canned meat.
19. One can of sardines.
20. Assorted energy bars, trail mix, nuts, and beef jerky.
21. Sixteen bar package of lifeboat rations (last resort food).
22. Ten single-serve coffee bags and sugar packages.[4]

Note: Food choices are just suggestions. Weight, space, and budget will dictate your selections, but food has to have a high priority for this

---

4   Use a vacuum sealer to further extend the shelf life of dried items.

long-term pack. Always have some foods that do not require cooking for situations where using a stove or starting a fire may not be practical.

Kits Packaged in Plastic Bags inside the Pack

These are items packaged in small nylon bags, pouches, or plastic bags.

Personal Sanitation Kit

1. Two ounces of liquid soap.
2. Two ounces of hand sanitizer.
3. Travel size toothpaste.
4. Toothbrush.
5. One or two razors.
6. One pair of latex gloves.
7. One large washcloth.
8. One 1.25 ounce insect repellant.
9. Nail clippers.
10. Small stainless steel camp mirror.
11. Toilet paper packets.

First Aid Kit

You can buy a commercially available kit or pack one of your own.

1. Assorted Bandages (Band-Aids™).
2. Hemostatic blood stopper gauze (various brands).
3. Four three-inch gauze pads.
4. Large wound dressing.
5. Eyewash (1.2 oz.).
6. Single edge razor blade.
7. Splinter tweezers.
8. Small scissors.
9. Neosporin or triple antibiotic cream.

10. Hydrocortisone cream.
11. Antacid tablets.
12. Laxative tablets.
13. Tylenol, Advil, etc.
14. Two pairs of latex gloves.
15. One roll of self-adhesive tape.
16. Tourniquet device such as the CAT™ or SWAT-T.

Sewing Kit

Like with the first aid kit, you can purchase a commercially available kit or compile one of your own making.

1. Assorted pins and safety pins.
2. Assorted needles.
3. Assorted small rolls of thread.
4. Assorted buttons.
5. Thimble.

Dental Repair Kit

You can purchase a toothache, filling, denture, and dental repair kit at pharmacies.

Fishing Kit

I recommend a Speed Hook™ fishing device or creating your own kit.

1. Assorted fish hooks.
2. Fishing line.
3. Assorted sinkers.
4. Two corks for floats.
5. Plastic worms and other lures.

Top row, left to right: Compact AR-7 rifle and slingshot, fit into the pack and provide practical hunting capability; freeze-dried food; pack; break-down bow and arrows.

Middle row, left to right: Documents; survival guide; personal hygiene items and a homemade first aid kit in the plastic bags; flair and flashlight; cooking utensils and cordage.

Bottom row, left to right: Black pouch containing Katadyn water purification system; light sticks; UVPaqlite; binoculars; radio; compact walkie-talkie; Garmin GPS navigation device. It is useful to add technology, but you should always have backup methods. I highly recommend redundancy in water purification, fire starting, shelter, defense, light, and nourishment.

Optional Items

1.   If you have a family or group participating in your survival plans and operations, have a good quality hand-held GMRS radio programmed to communicate with your other group members.
2.   You can have one or all three of the weapons listed below. They take up little room and add only a few pounds— total—to your pack.
     •   The Henry Arms AR-7, .22 caliber, Survival Rifle with the bulky, floating stock replaced with a compact folding stock. And 200 to 300 rounds of ammunition.
     •   A five-piece, breakdown survival bow such as the Nomad™ with six to twelve arrows.
     •   A small slingshot with some steel ball bearing ammunition.

Hybrid Packs and Kits

In reality, a "survival pack" can be any combination of container and contents that meets your needs under your specific, anticipated emergency situation. It can be a combination of items from any and all of the above lists, carried in bags, packs, pockets, and vests of any kind. The objective is to have what you need, where you need it, when you need it.

While having more is usually better, extra weight and bulk may prohibit your ability to carry your supplies to where you need them and it may slow your escape from harm. Survival is not a picnic or a camping trip. You may need to sacrifice comfort and nice-to-have items for more of the essentials and for your ability to carry them. A few examples of hybrid survival packs are as follows:

- You may need to carry more of the long-term pack items such as food and shelter in a survival kit if your outdoor activities take you further away from civilization.
- While the basic FEMA evacuation pack provides food for three days, you may elect to expand that and other contents if you are concerned that an emergency could make you a refugee for a longer period of time.
- You may want to combine the elements of a Get Home Pack and an Evacuation Pack in case you can't get home or it takes longer than expected.
- If weight is a serious issue, you can replace some of the heavier and bulkier items in the Bugout pack with the lighter options from the Survival Kit and Evacuation Bag. Replacing the cooked foods with all ready-to-eat foods eliminates the need for a stove and fuel. An ultra-light sleeping bag and a Space Blanket™ can replace a full sized sleeping bag. Such sacrifices will make finding shelter, building a fire, and foraging for food more necessary, but will facilitate your rapid movement.

A realistic evaluation of what type of emergencies you will face, how long these emergencies will continue, and under what conditions they will exist will determine what kind of pack you elect to assemble. Ideally, a few overnight hikes and camping trips using just what's in your pack or kit will proved an accurate concept of what you truly need and what you can actually carry.

Appendix: Book List

RECOMMENDED BOOKS

I am frequently asked, "What books would you recommend for me to learn more about survival?" After forty years of study, many of the books I started with are out of print. I have a few hundred on the shelves and more in tote bins. I tend not to buy the newest books because most of the information is already on my shelves. Since there is such a great variety of survival concerns and every person and family will have a unique set of attitudes and challenges, there can be no one or two books that will contain everything someone would need to know. Some books are dry manuals, others are pure data, and some contain survival information in a narrative or as a novel. You should seek out the information that fits your greatest concerns and is the most readable and understandable. This list is not a complete catalog and will continue to change as newer publications are added and others are deleted.

General Survival Preparedness and Self-Reliance

Back to Basics edited by Abigail R. Gehring. A very well-illustrated and organized book that covers many basic rural self-reliance subjects, including gardening, well digging, food preservation, raising chickens, sheep, and goats, and many other skills. 450 pages, 8½ x 11 inches, hardcover, $27.95 from Skyhorse Publishing. www.skyhorsepublishing.com

The Ultimate Guide to U.S. Army Survival: Skills, Tactics, and Techniques edited by Jay McCullough. Actually a reprint of rearrangement of US Army survival manuals. This is a very large black and white illustrated manual covering outdoor survival, first aid, navigation, fire craft, combat, shelter building, and much more. 953 pages, 8½ x 11 inches, paperback, $24.99 from Skyhorse Publishing. www.skyhorsepublishing.com

Advanced Survival by James C. Jones. This book covers basic alternative methods of replacing each essential survival need and service now provided by our public utilities, services, and business. Included are methods to provide food, clean water, sanitation, protection, transportation, and all other necessities of life when the grid fails. 191 pages, 5½ x 8¼ inches, paperback, $16.99 from Skyhorse Publishing. www.skyhorsepublishing.com

Total Survival by James C. Jones. Ten ways to gather and purify water, ten ways to survive street crime, ten ways to find or make a shelter, ten ways to procure and preserve food, and ten methods for dealing with many more survival needs. Illustrated with drawings and photographs. 8½ x 11 inches, 179 pages, paperback, $16.99 from Skyhorse Publishing. www.skyhorsepublishing.com

150 Survival Secrets by James C. Jones. One hundred and fifty survival-related issues addressed in a question and answer format. Many critical and controversial issues are included in this comprehensive survival manual and survivalist manifesto. 282 pages, 6 x 9 inches, paperback, $17.99 from Skyhorse Publishing. www.skyhorsepublishing.com

The Complete Guide to Edible Wild Plants. Originally created as a US Army manual. This book covers identification and location of common edible wild plants and how to prepare them as food. 149 pages, 6 x 9 inches, paperback, $12.95 from Skyhorse Publishing. www.skyhorsepublishing.com

The Survivalist's Handbook by Rainer Stahlberg. Equipment lists, food storage plans, and much more. Scenarios are covered on what to do on day one, day two, day three, etc. Disaster plans include what to do in case of fire, flood, nuclear disaster, epidemic, tornadoes, and even volcano eruptions. 430 pages, 5 x 7 inches, paperback, $14.95 from Skyhorse Publishing. www.skyhorsepublishing.com

Living off The Grid by David Black. Basic information on alternative sources of water, electricity, heat, food, and other necessities when the grid goes down. 253 pages, 5 x 7½ inches, paperback, $12.95 from Skyhorse Publishing. www.skyhorsepublishing.com

Everyday Survival Kits by Mark Puhaly and Joel Stevens. Urban "bug out bags," day hike kits, car kits, cold weather kits, everyday kits and more. 182 pages, 5½ x 8 inches, paperback, $17.99 from Living Ready Books. www.livingreadyonline.com

Preppers Food Storage by Julie Languille. A well-organized book on how to set up a survival food storage system. Includes charts and calculation tables on nutritional needs and shelf life. 255 pages, 6 x 9 inches, paperback, $12.95 from Ulysses Publications. www.ulyssespublications.com

Peterson Field Guide to Medicinal Plants and Herbs of Eastern and Central America by Steven Foster and James A. Duke. This book covers 530 of the most common medicinal and edible plants in the central and eastern United States. Color illustrations. 456 pages, paperback, $21.00 from HMH Books. www.hmhco.com

52 Prepper Projects by David Nash. Well-described and illustrated projects that you can do with minimal tools and materials that can improve your survival potential. Fun and easy tasks to help prepare you for the unpredictable. 198 pages, 6 x 9 inches, paperback, $16.95 from Skyhorse Publishing. www.skyhorsepublishing.com

100 Deadly Survival Skills by Clint Emerson. A clearly illustrated manual of Seal and CIA survival tricks and techniques. Lots of improvised methods that could save your life. Only a few are deadly. 256 pages, 5½ x 8½ inches, paperback, $19.99 from Simon and Shuster. www.simonandshusterpublishing.com

Soldiers of Fortune Guide to Surviving the Apocalypse by N. E. Mac-Dougald. Covers a number of survival situations and survival techniques in well-written and illustrated chapters. 193 pages, 6 x 9 inches, paperback, $14.95 from Skyhorse Publishing. www.skyhorsepublishing.com

The Complete SAS Survival Manual by Barry Davies. This book includes escape and evasion, navigation, shelter, self-defense, and much more. Fully illustrated in color. 276 pages, 6½ x 9¼ inches, paperback, $14.95 from Skyhorse Publishing. www.skyhorsepublishing.com

SAS and Elite Forces Guide Preparing to Survive by Chris McNab. Everything from home bunkers, home security, street combat, and nuclear war survival to wilderness survival and first aid and combat techniques. 320 pages, 5 x 7 inches, paperback, $19.95 from Lyons Press. www.LyonsPress.com

What to Do When the Shit Hits the Fan by David Black. Basic preparedness and survival techniques for most natural and manmade disaster situations. Includes how to survive terrorist attacks, fire, floods, tornadoes, earthquakes, civil unrest, and many other situations are covered. 290 pages, 5 x 7 inches, $12.95 from Skyhorse Publishing. www.skyhorsepublishing.com

Prepper's Communication Handbook by Jim Cobb. Lifesaving strategies for communicating with family and group members when the phone systems and Internet fail. Includes use and limitations of satellite phone, GMRS, FRS, CB, VHF, etc. 132 pages, 6 x 9 inches, paperback, $15.95 from Ulysses Publications. www.ulyssespress.com

The Pocket Guide to Prepping Supplies by Patty Hahne. Lists and evaluates over 200 items that you need to be prepared. Covers details on storage methods, what to carry, shelving, and packs. 156 pages, 4¼ x 6¼ inches, paperback, $9.99 from Skyhorse Publishing. www.skyhorsepublishing.com

The Prepper's Water Survival Guide by Daisy Luther. How to gather, purify, and store water before and during survival emergencies. 216 pages, 6 x 9 inches, paperback, $14.95 from Ulysses Publications. www.ulyssespress.com

Bug Out by Scott Williams. A well-written book on how to plan and equip for escape and evacuation from various kinds of disasters. Covers motor vehicles, boats, bicycles, and foot travel. 301 pages, 6 x 9 inches, paperback, $14.95 from Ulysses Publications. www.ulyssespress.com

How To Survive Anywhere by Christopher Nyerges. Written by a very experienced survival school instructor, this book covers survival techniques for forest, desert, coastal, and cold weather environments with plenty of good advice, clear illustrations, and photographs. 264 pages, 5½ x 8¼ inches, $19.95 from Stackpole Books. www.stackpolebooks.com

Self-Sufficiency for the 21st Century by Dick and James Strawbridge. One of the best all-around self-reliance instructional books you can buy. If you are planning on moving beyond basic survival to full self-sufficiency this is the one book you should start with. Covers all aspects of food production, water harvesting, alternative energy, and much more. Extremely well-illustrated and written. 304 pages, 7½ x 9 inches, paperback, $22.95 from Penguin Random House. www.penguinrandomhouse.com

The Survival Food Handbook by Janet Groene. The author bases her recommendations on her extensive experiences in stocking boats for long voyages and from wilderness camping. There is a glossary of shelf-stable foods and her own "top thirteen foods for storage." This is a great little book for survival preparedness and wilderness camping. 154 pages, 6 x 9 inches, paperback, $20.00 from International Marine. www.mhprofessional.com/international-marine

Outdoor & Wilderness Survival

How to Survive Anything, Anywhere by Chris McNab. A well-illustrated readable manual that covers outdoor survival, survival psychology, kits, and some urban survival situations. A very good starter manual. 320 pages, 7 x 9 inches, paperback $21.00 from International Marine. www.mhprofessional.com/international-marine

The Encyclopedia of Survival Techniques by Alexander Stilwell. A nicely illustrated outdoor survival manual covering survival techniques by region. Desert, tropics, polar, and mountain survival are well covered. There are sections on natural disasters and first aid as well. 192 pages, 7 x 9 inches, paperback, $19.95 from The Lyons Press. www.lyonspress.com

SAS Survival Guide (Collins Gem Edition) by John "Lofty" Wiseman. This miniature book is loaded with information on food, water, shelter, navigation, first aid, shelter construction, and other survival skills. A must for your pack. 384 pages, 3 x 4 inches, paperback, $8.00 from Harper Collins Publishing. www.harpercollins.com

Wilderness Survival by Gregory J. Davenport. A well-illustrated manual on basic outdoor survival techniques. 129 pages, 5½ x 8¼ inches, paperback, $21.95 from Stackpole Books. www.stackpolebooks.com

Surviving Cold Weather by Gregory Davenport. Lots of photos and drawings to illustrate the hazards and techniques of cold weather. 240 pages, 5½ x 8¼ inches, paperback, $14.95 from Stackpole Books. www.stackpolebooks.com.

The Complete Survival Shelters Handbook by Anthonio Akkermans. Step-by-step instructions to building shelters for every climate and location with what is available. 144 pages, 7½ x 9¼ inches, paperback, $15.95 from Ulysses Publications. www.ulyssespress.com

Bushcraft by Richard Graves. A well-written and illustrated handbook on all aspects of outdoor survival including fire, water, shelter, navigation, trapping, fishing, and much more. 344 pages, 5½ x 8¼ inches, paperback, $16.95 from Skyhorse Publishing. www.skyhorsepublishing.com

Urban Survival & Self Protection

Defend Yourself by Rob Pincus. With color photographs, this book covers passive home security devices and techniques, defensive weapons selection, and use. Special attention is given to armed defensive combat with handguns, shotguns, and rifles. 248 pages, 6 x 9 inches, paperback, $10.00 from Gun Digest Books. www.gundigeststore.com/books-resources

Urban Emergency Survival Plan by Jim Cobb. This book covers how to survive a variety of disasters in an urban environment. It includes what to do when the electricity, sanitation, water supply, and food sources are interrupted and civil disorder and chaos reign. 176 pages, 6 x 9 inches, paperback, $17.99 from Living Ready Books. www.livingreadyonline.com

SAS Urban Survival Handbook by John Wiseman. A good survival and safety manual for anyone living in town. The book covers a lot of basic home and street safety information as well as emergency plans and disaster survival. There are some well-illustrated self-defense techniques and lots of information on crime prevention. 316 pages, 6 x 9 inches, paperback, $20.00 from Harper Collins publishers. www.harpercollins.com

Ragnar's Urban Survival by Ragnar Benson. A good manual for those who would stay in an urban area under desperate circumstances. Covers ways to forage, find water, avoid troops and gangs, and much more. 200 pages, 5½ x 8¼ inches, paperback, $20.00 from Paladin Press. www.paladin.press.com

How to be Safe by Ira L. Chapman. Written by the founder of Guardsmark LLC, one of the nation's largest private security firms, this book focuses on crime prevention and travel safety on the personal and business level. Well-written and easy to use. 359 pages, 5 x 9 inches, hardcover, $10.50 from Amazon. www.amazon.com

Military Manuals

Survival Evasion and Escape by the Department of the Army. The original "survival manual." This military manual covers outdoor survival under a wide variety of conditions such as arctic, swamp, jungle, desert, and ocean environments. Lots of information on water sources, edible plants, trapping, and shelters. 288 pages, 6 x 9 inches, paperback, $14.95 from Barnes & Noble. www.barnesandnoble.com

The U.S. Armed Forces Nuclear, Biological and Chemical Survival Manual by Dick Couch, USNR Captain, retired. Not an official government printed manual, but a good overview manual on NBC survival. 242 pages, 5½ x 8¼ inches, paperback, $14.95 from Basic Books. www.basicbooks.com

U.S. Air Force Survival Handbook by the United States Air Force. A military manual covering a wide range of outdoor and military survival skills including shelter building, navigation, trapping, mountaineering, edible plants, and much more. 575 pages, 8½ x 11 inches, paperback, $17.99 from Skyhorse Publishing. www.skyhorsepublishing.com

General Preparedness and Self-Reliance

Dare to Prepare by Holly Drennan Deyo. A fully indexed and illustrated home preparedness manual, including scores of data tables on food requirements, food storage, fuel needs, etc. A must have. 624 pages, 8 x 11 inches, paperback, $39.00 from Dayo Enterprises LLC. www.daretoprepare.com

Back to Basics edited by Abigail R. Gehring. An extremely well-illustrated and narrated how-to guide to twenty-six basic self-reliance skills. Subjects include keeping bees, milking cows, planting gardens, canning, pickling, preserving, and using natural energy (wind, water, sun), and much more. The perfect book for anyone trying to become more self-sufficient. 456 pages, 9 x 11 inches, hardcover, $27.95 from Skyhorse Publishing. www.skyhorsepublishing.com

Living off the Land in the City and Country by Ragnar Benson. While not covering everything, it does have a lot of information on self-reliance that can be used in most environments. 270 pages, 5½ x 8¼ inches, paperback, $14.99 from Paladin Press. www.paladin.press.com

Wilderness Living by Gregory Davenport. Basic information for those contemplating retreating to the backcountry. 240 pages, 5½ x 8¼ inches, paperback, $19.95 from Stackpole books. www.stackpolebooks.com

Survival Combat

Combat Leader's Field Guide by Jeff Kirkham. A compact combination survival manual and combat guide. Covers navigation, tactics, field fortification, weapons, first aid, and more. 268 pages, 4 x 6 inches, paperback, $12.95 from Stackpole books. www.stackpolebooks.com

The Ultimate Guide to U.S. Army Combat Skills, Tactics, and Techniques edited by Jay McCullough. Reprinted US army training manual covers tactics, weapons, self-defense, field craft, camouflage, fortification, and movement. 960 pages, 8½ x 11 inches, paperback, $24.95 from Skyhorse Publishing. www.skyhorsepublishing.com

Aid and Emergency Medicine

US Army Special Forces Medical Handbook by Glen K. Craig. Diagnostic and treatment instructions for a wide variety of medical emergencies. Includes primitive medicine, veterinary medicine, and obstetrics. 608 pages, 4¼ x 7 inches, paperback, $30.00 from Paladin Press. www.paladin.press.com

Tactical Combat Care and Wound Management by the US Department of Defense. This is a well-illustrated medical care manual focused on combat field trauma such as burns, soft tissue injures, fractures, penetrations, and evulsions. 175 pages, 6 x 9 inches, paperback, $16.99 from Skyhorse Publishing. www.skyhorsepublishing.com

Emergency War Surgery by the Department of the Army. A revision of a NATO handbook, this volume covers advanced techniques for care of wounds, burns, chemical, and blast injuries, and much more. 488 pages, 5½ x 8¼ inches, paperback, $29.99 from Skyhorse Publishing. www.skyhorsepublishing.com

Special Operations Forces Medical Handbook by US Department of Defense. A revision of a Defense Department Handbook. Extensive and detailed information on medication dosages, dental procedures, child delivery, veterinary medicine, and much more. 688 pages, 5½ x 8¼ inches, paperback, $16.95 from Skyhorse Publishing. www.skyhorsepublishing.com

Do It Yourself Medicine by Ragnar Benson. Includes ways to find and use various antibiotics and anesthetics without prescriptions. Necessary information as the medical care system collapses. 126 pages, 5½ x 8¼ inches, paperback, $13.50 from Paladin Press. www.paladin.press.com

Prepper's Survival Medicine Handbook by Scott Finazzo. A well-illustrated first aid handbook that also covers some basic survival issues and includes information on biological and radiological medical care. 192 pages, 6 x 9 inches, paperback, $15.95 from Ulysses Press. www.ulyssespress.com

The Merck Manual of Medical Information (Home Edition) by Mark H. Beers. Thoroughly indexed to cover virtually all medical conditions and injuries, by symptom. Covers all medications and techniques. This is the one your doctor uses! 1767 pages, 4 x 7 inches, hardcover, $9.99 from Pocket Books. www.simonandschusterpublishing.com

Survival Story Novels (Fiction & Nonfiction)

Note: I am not including any "survival novels" that are just for recreation. These books have heavy content of practical information or tactical lessons.

Defiance by Nechama Tec and Edward Zwick. This is the story of how Jews who fled from cities under Nazi occupation in Poland during World War II we able to escape, evade, resist, and survive for years in the Nalibocka Forest. They established a fully functional survival camp with shops, infirmaries, schools, and a military force in "defiance" of all attempts to exterminate them. Stuff other books only guess about. 369 pages, 5½ x 8¼ inches, paperback, $9.99 from Oxford Press. www.global.oup.com

Patriots by James Wesley Rawles. A multifaceted novel of people and families escaping and surviving a general collapse of civilization. Scenarios include long foot-marches through hostile country, establishment and defense of a well-stocked survival retreat, and the reestablishment of community security and self-reliance. The book is heavy on philosophy and detailed data on how to do things and what to have. A highly readable story and a manual combined. 400 pages, 6 x 9 inches, paperback, $14.95 from Ulysses Press. www.ulyssespress.com

Survival Psychology

Deep Survival by Laurence Gonzales. This book uses true stories of endurance and survival to illustrate how people think under stress and what kinds of mental techniques and philosophies work.

Highly readable and highly educational. 299 pages, 6 x 9½ inches, hardcover, $25.95 from W. W. Norton & Company. www.wwnorton.com

Surviving Survival by Laurence Gonzales. The author follows up the cases from his *Deep Survival* book by exploring the effects of disaster on the individual psyche months and years later. Although people did survive the original disaster or attack they often suffered disastrous mental debilitation. Why do some people shrug off horrible events while others are traumatized to the point of suicide? 250 pages, 6 x 8½ inches, hardcover, $15.95 from W. W. Norton & Company. www.wwnorton.com

The Survivors Club by Ben Sherwood. The secrets and science of survival that could save your life. An in-depth study of how people react to emergencies and disaster situations. Details the mental attitudes and propensities of those who are most likely to survive. The book includes a link to an online test that analyzes your survival strengths and weakness. 383 pages, 5½ x 9 inches, paperback, $16.99 from Penguin Books. www.penguin.com

Collapse by Jared Diamond. A Pulitzer Prize winning author and professor of geography uses historic examples and scientific data to predict the inevitable and already in progress collapse of civilization as we know it. This is THE most compelling argument for survival preparedness. 573 pages, 5½ x 8¼ inches, paperback, $12.99 from Penguin Books. www.penguin.com

The Unthinkable by Amanda Ripley. An in-depth analysis of how people respond to disasters. The author takes us through the experiences of people who have survived a variety of real disasters to illustrate how the mind goes through three stages before acting to survive. The book explores why some people freeze and die while others act and live. 265 pages, 6 x 9½ inches, hardcover, $24.95 from Crown Publishing. www.crownpublishing.com

The Gray Rhino by Michele Wucker. Not a traditional "survival" book, but very relevant to understanding how and why we fail to recognize and react to impending disasters. The book explores why the individual, society, and governments are blinded to the obvious (charging rhino's) multiple and unavoidable catastrophes of the future. It also explains the unpopularity and frustration of preparedness advocates. 252 pages, 6 x 9½ inches, paperback, $20.99 from St. Martin's Press. www.us.macmillan.com/smp

Survivors by John B. Letterman. Twenty-three of the most brutal tales of true survival known to man. Starting with the epic journey of Alvar Nunez Cabeza de Vaca who was stranded in Florida in 1528 and managed to reach Spanish colonies in Texas in 1536 and moving through shipwrecks, arctic expeditions, POW escapes, to modern air crashes. 460 pages, 6 x 9½ inches, hardcover, $7.99 from Simon & Schuster. www.simonandschusterpublishing.com

The SAS Mental Endurance Handbook by Chris McNab. Based on various British Army methods for staying focused and handling stress. Includes illustrated tests and examples. A good section on surviving prison camp. 190 pages, 7 x 9 inches, paperback, $19.95 from The Lyons Press. www.lyonspress.com

About the Author

James. C. Jones was born on the Southside of Chicago at the beginning of World War II. An impoverished and chaotic childhood made him a natural survivalist from a very early age. He put together his own survival pack at age twelve and often spent time in the woodlands and swaps that adjoined the city at that time. Working two jobs while living in a one-room apartment and attending high school in the tough Southside added more real world survival experiences. Starting as a technician at a large chemical manufacturing complex, his passion for safety led him to become an award winning safety manager. While acquiring certifications in emergency medicine, hazardous chemical handling, safety management, and training management related to his job, he energetically pursued survival related activities including rock climbing, caving, rafting, horseback riding, and survival camping. He founded Live Free USA in the late 1960s and helped it evolve from an outdoor survival club into a broad based, national preparedness and self-reliance education organization. During the 1970s and 1980s he was a leading voice in defending and defining responsible survivalism on national television and radio and even the BBC.

James C. Jones is the author of *Advanced Survival, Total Survival,* and *150 Survival Secrets* published by Skyhorse Publishing. He has developed and conducted hundreds of survival training events and seminars over the past forty years and has written hundreds of articles for Live Free's newsletter as well as American Survivor's newsletter and website at www.americansurvivor.org. He is now retired and living in Indiana, but currently writes articles for several national preparedness and survival related publications, while continuing to teach a variety of survival courses and make presentations at major preparedness expositions. He may be contacted at survivorjj@aol.com.

Directory of Survival and Preparedness Supply Sources

Supplier	Website	Phone #	Stores and Catalogs	Goods and Products
Sportsman's Guide	SportsmansGuide.com	1-800-888-3006	Online and catalog sales	Offers a variety of new and surplus military packs, clothing, sleeping bags, tents, and other gear.
Cabela's	Cabelas.com	N/A	Online and in stores located throughout the US, catalogs on request	In-store and online sales of camping, shooting, sporting, and outdoor survival items.
CH Kadel's	CHKADELS.com	1-800-735-8001	Online and catalog sales	Offers a large selection of survival related products.
ReadyMan Products	Readyman.com	1-385-267-9710	Online only	A unique line of compact survival, defense, and escape products.

Supplier	Website	Phone #	Stores and Catalogs	Goods and Products
US Patriot Tactical	uspatriottactical.com	N/A	Online only	A full line of high-quality survival gear for civilian, police, and military applications.
5ive Star Gear	5ivestargear.com	N/A	Online and through dealers	A good selection of outdoor clothing, police supplies, packs, safety items, and survival items.
Survival-Supply.com	Survival-Supply.com	N/A	Online only	A very complete selection of need-specific survival and first aid kits, fire extinguishers, and more.
ReadyWise LLC	Readywise.com Wisecompany.com	800-820-1329	Online or by phone	Survival foods, prepackaged packs and kits, more.
RedCross Store.com	RedCrossStore.com	N/A	Online only	Basic first aid and emergency kits.
Titan Survival	titansurvival.com	N/A	Online only	Cordage, emergency shelters, fire-starters, and other survival items.
Major Surplus and Survival	Majorsurplus.com	1-800-441-8855	Online and catalog sales	A full line of clothing, camping, disaster preparedness, and tactical gear.
Tactical Gear Super Store	Tacticalgear.com	N/A	Online only	Clothing, packs, survival tools, fire starters, and knives.
SOG (Special Ops Gear)	Sogknives.com	N/A	Online and through dealers	Knives, hatchets, multitools, fire starters, packs, and more.

Supplier	Website	Phone #	Stores and Catalogs	Goods and Products
Rescue Essentials	Rescue-Essentials.com	N/A	Online only	Advanced medical care equipment, chest seals, decompression needles, airways, splints, trauma kits.
Nitro-Pak	Nitro-pak.com	N/A	Online only	A very complete line of survival and advanced medical supplies, including surgical kits, water purification systems, survival foods, packs, tools, and sanitation items.
BUDK	BUDK.com	1-800-543-5016	Online and catalog sales	Various survival devices, knives, antibiotics, lock picks, etc.
Gerber	Gerbergear.com	N/A	Online and through dealers	Knives, axes, multi-tools, and machetes.
Garman	Garmen.com	1-800-721-1373	Online and through dealers	GPS navigation devices and radios.
NRA Store	nrastore.com nratactical.com	N/A	Online only	Shooting accessories, survival gear, tools, packs, and clothing.
REI	Rei.com	1-800-426-4840	Online and through dealers	Camping gear, tents, sleeping bags, knives, climbing gear, packs, and topographical maps.
Midland	Mid.factoryoutletstore .com	1-855-896-0051	Online and through dealers	Emergency radios and walkie-talkies.

Supplier	Website	Phone #	Stores and Catalogs	Goods and Products
Smith & Wesson	Smith-wesson.com	N/A	Online and through dealers	Firearms and knives.
The Prepper Stop	Theprepperstop.com	N/A	Online only	Radiological monitoring gear, solar chargers, and more.
Live Free Outfitters	LiveFreeOutfitters.com/Survival	312-500-5130	Online and by phone	Survival items with a discount to Live Free members.
Patriot Outfitters	Patriotoutfitters.com	N/A	Online only	Packs, knives, first aid kits, and clothing.
Optics Planet	Opticsplanet.com	N/A	Online only	Binoculars, scopes, and night vision equipment.
Radmeters4u	Radmeters4u.com	1-830-672-8734	Online only	New and surplus radiation detectors.
Mountain House	Mountainhouse.com	N/A	Online and through dealers	Freeze-dried foods.
Skyhorse Publishing	Skyhorsepublishing.com	N/A	Online and through dealers	Survival and self-reliance books.
Survival Warehouse	Survival-warehouse.com	N/A	Online only	Survival kits, gear, sleeping bags, stoves, and freeze-dried foods.
Solkoa Survival Systems	Solkoasurvival.com.	1-719-634-1587	Online Only	Specialized survival kits and equipment.
MRE Star	Mre-meals.net	N/A	Online and through dealers	Meals Ready to Eat (MREs).
RDD USA	Rddusa.com	N/A	Online only	Complete selection of gas masks and military surplus gear.

Supplier	Website	Phone #	Stores and Catalogs	Goods and Products
Ultimate Survival Technologies	Ultimatesurvival.com	N/A	Online only	Prepackaged survival kits and a variety of survival gear.
Elite Ops Energy Strips	EliteOpsPower.com/ Survival	312-500-5130	Online and through dealers	Emergency energy products.
Northern Safety	Northernsafety.com	1-800-571-4646	Online and catalog sales	Chemical protective clothing and respirators.
Granger	Granger.com	1-800-472-4643	Online and catalog sales	Chemical protective clothing and respirators.
Emergency Essentials	Beprepared.com	1-800-999-1863	Online and by phone	Long-term survival food packages and systems.
Galls	Galls.com	866-673-7643	Online and catalog sales	Police and public safety equipment.
Best Sharpening Stones	Bestsharpeningstones.com	N/A	Online only	Sharpening stones.
Emergency Kits.com	Emergencykits.com	N/A	Online only	Emergency and disaster survival items, and sanitation kits.
Legacy Emergency Foods	Legacyfoodstorage.com	N/A	Online only	Freeze-dried foods for camping and emergencies.
LPD Camping Foods	Lpdcampingfoods.com	1-800-826-5767	Online only	Freeze-dried foods for camping and emergencies.
Colman	Colman.com	N/A	Online and through dealers	Stoves, lanterns, tents, and camping gear.
Live Action Safty	Liveactionsafety.com	N/A	Online only	Medical kits and safety gear.
UV Paqlite	Uvpaqlite.com	N/A	Online only	A variety of self-charging, glow-in-the-dark products for emergency use.
Edgemaker	Edgemaker.com	1-800-532-3343	Online only	Sharpening devices.

Supplier	Website	Phone #	Stores and Catalogs	Goods and Products
Blade Headquarters	Bladehq.com	N/A	Online only	Specializes in survival and combat knives.
Hustle Paint Ball	Hustlepaintball.com	N/A	Online only	Smoke bombs.
West Marine	Westmarine.com	N/A	Online only	Flairs and flair guns.
Widgetco	Widgetco.com	N/A	Online only	Silica-gel desiccant.
Uline	Uline.com	1-800-295-5510	Online only	Silica-gel desiccant.
Spreetail	Spreetail.com	N/A	Online and through dealers	Rubber boats.
Forge Survival Supply	Forgesurvivalsupply.com	N/A	Online only	Survival packs, food, and gear.
Safe Castle	Safecastle.com	N/A	Online only	Survival kits, packs, food, and gear.
My Medic	MyMedic.com	N/A	Online only	First aid kits and tourniquets.
RATS	RATSmedical.com	N/A	Online only	RATS tourniquets.
The Apprentice Doctor	Theapprenticedoctor.com	N/A	Online only	Suturing training kits, IV training kits, etc.
AR-7.com	ar7.rifles.imoutdoorshostring.com	N/A	Online only	Folding stocks, magazines, and parts for AR-7 rifles.
Customized Accessories	ar-7.com	N/A	Online only	Folding stocks, magazines, and parts for AR-7 rifles.
Surviv-alSlingshot.com	SurvivalSlingshot.com	N/A	Online only	Survival slingshots.
KnifeCenter.com	KnifeCenter.com	N/A	Online only	Wide selection of knives.